interchange

THIRD EDITION

Jack C. Richards
with *Jonathan Hull, Susan Proctor,*
Kate Cory-Wright, Elena Dorado,
and Sérgio Piancó

TEACHER'S RESOURCE BOOK

2

CAMBRIDGE UNIVERSITY PRESS
Cambridge, New York, Melbourne, Madrid, Cape Town, Singapore, São Paulo

Cambridge University Press
40 West 20th Street, New York, NY 10011-4211, USA

www.cambridge.org
Information on this title: www.cambridge.org/9780521602044

First published 2005

Printed in Hong Kong, China

A catalog record for this publication is available from the British Library

ISBN-13 978-0-521-60204-4 paperback
ISBN-10 0-521-60204-1 paperback

Art direction, book design, photo research, and layout services: Adventure House, NYC
Audio production: Richard LePage & Associates

Illustrations:
Adolar de Paula Mendes Filho: 1–9, 11–19, 22, 25, 28
Andrew Shiff: 71, 74, 75, 81, 82, 83, 84

Photography:
69 © Punchstock
70 © Corbis
72 © Jacques Copeau/Getty Images
73 (*left to right*) © Piotr Powietrzynski/age fotostock; © Getty Images
76 © Chris Hondros/Getty Images
77 (*both photos*) © Bettmann/Corbis
78 © Bob Daemmrich/PhotoEdit
79 (*left*) © Alamy; (*top right*) © Photos.com; (*bottom right*) © Alamy
80 (*left to right*) © Puttnam/Topical Press Agency/Getty Images; © Yellow Dog Productions/Getty Images

Contents

Introduction

The *Interchange Third Edition Teacher's Resource Book 2* is a rich source of easy-to-use supplementary materials for review and reinforcement of the language and skills taught in *Interchange Third Edition Student's Book 2*. It is based on feedback and suggestions provided by teachers around the world. The book consists of the following sections:

- **Listening** Additional listening activities develop a wide variety of listening skills, including listening for gist, listening for details, and inferring meaning from context. There is one photocopiable Listening page for each unit of the Student's Book.

- **Grammar** Activities in this section reinforce the grammar introduced and practiced in the Student's Book. There is one photocopiable Grammar page for each unit. Each page includes two activities, one for written practice and the other one for oral practice. The written activities can be used either in class or for homework.

- **Vocabulary** There is a photocopiable vocabulary log for each unit of the Student's Book. The first exercise, *Your Vocabulary Log*, allows learners to record new words from the unit so that they remember them better. The second exercise, *Practice*, consists of an activity for reviewing the key vocabulary from the unit.

- **Writing** This section includes additional writing practice for each unit of the Student's Book. The Writing pages provide complete teaching sequences, from analyzing a model, brainstorming and organizing ideas for a first draft, editing the draft, to final revision.

- **Projects** This section includes a wide range of new ways to extend the main topics, both in and out of the classroom. There is one project for each unit. Detailed teaching notes for each project are on pages 65–68.

- **Answer Keys** This section provides answers for the Listening, Grammar, Vocabulary, and Writing exercises. It also contains audio scripts for the Listening section.

INTERVIEW ABOUT THE PAST

A *Pair work* Daniel interviewed Huang and Pedro about their past.
What questions do you think he asked?

Huang

Pedro

B ▶ Listen to the interviews. Check (✓) True (T) or False (F).

Huang	T	F
1. Huang moved to Canada when she was a teenager.	☐	☐
2. She has some nice memories of Vietnam.	☐	☐
3. She was good at music as a child.	☐	☐
4. Her first piano was a very good one.	☐	☐
5. Her father was musical.	☐	☐

Pedro	T	F
1. Pedro wanted to be a chef when he was younger.	☐	☐
2. He couldn't find a teaching job after he graduated.	☐	☐
3. His first job was as a waiter in a restaurant.	☐	☐
4. He opened a restaurant five years ago.	☐	☐
5. His business has been quite slow.	☐	☐

C ▶ Listen again. Answer the questions.

Huang

1. Where did her mother use to work? _____

2. Where did she use to take piano lessons? _____

3. When did she give her first concert? _____

Pedro

1. What did he use to play? _____

2. Who first taught him to cook? _____

3. Who did he use to watch at work? _____

D *Pair work* Write four questions to ask your partner about his or her past.
Interview your partner.

CITY PROBLEMS

A *Pair work* Look at the pictures. Do you have these problems in your city or town? What other problems are there?

dangerous crosswalks

air pollution

traffic jams

B ▶ Listen to the conversations about problems in a city. Number the pictures from 1 to 3.

C ▶ Listen again. Check (✔) the two solutions suggested for each problem.

1. ☐ a. Move factories away from the city.
   ☐ b. Move away from the factories.
   ☐ c. Fine the companies responsible.

2. ☐ a. Keep trucks out of cities during rush hour.
   ☐ b. Don't allow cars with only one person.
   ☐ c. Improve the subway and bus system.

3. ☐ a. Fine drivers who don't stop.
   ☐ b. Add more traffic lights.
   ☐ c. Add more crosswalks.

D *Pair work* Discuss ways to solve the problems you chose in part A.

© Cambridge University Press   Photocopiable

HOW DID YOU LIKE THE APARTMENT?

A *Group work* Mark and Louise are apartment hunting. Read the list of things they want. Add two things that you want. Compare your ideas.

B ▷ Listen to Mark and Louise discuss the apartments they visited. Check (✓) True (T) or False (F).

1.   **T**   **F**

1. The kitchen is large.   ☐   ☐
2. There aren't enough bedrooms.   ☐   ☐
3. It doesn't have enough furniture.   ☐   ☐
4. It's too expensive.   ☐   ☐

2.   **T**   **F**

1. The living room is too small.   ☐   ☐
2. The living room is too dark.   ☐   ☐
3. The kitchen isn't big enough.   ☐   ☐
4. There aren't enough bedrooms.   ☐   ☐

C ▷ Listen again. How much is the rent for each apartment? What is the neighborhood like? Complete the chart.

	Rent	Neighborhood
1.		
2.		

D *Group work* Which apartment would you choose? Give reasons for your choice.

HOW DO YOU MAKE THAT DISH?

A *Pair work* Some people are having dinner. Three people brought these dishes. What do you think they are? What do you think is in them? Compare ideas.

B ▶ Listen to the conversations at dinner. Number the dishes from 1 to 3.

C ▶ Listen again. Check (✓) True (T) or False (F).

1.	T	F
1. This dish takes a long time to prepare.	☐	☐
2. You need fresh chicken or beef.	☐	☐
3. You cook the vegetables for three or four minutes.	☐	☐
4. You add the sauce or spices at the end.	☐	☐

2.	T	F
1. The man makes his own dough for the crust.	☐	☐
2. You need some tomato sauce.	☐	☐
3. You fry the dough in olive oil.	☐	☐
4. You bake it for about 20 minutes.	☐	☐

3.	T	F
1. The bread crumbs add flavor.	☐	☐
2. The woman doesn't make her own sauce.	☐	☐
3. You fry the onions and garlic.	☐	☐
4. You cook these in sauce for about 40 minutes.	☐	☐

D *Group work* Plan a party. Decide what dish each person will bring. Describe the ingredients in the dish and explain how to make it.

SUMMER BREAK

A *Pair work* Look at the picture of a summer camp. What activities are the children doing? What other activities do children do at summer camp?

B ▶ Listen to John and Maria talk about their summer plans. Check (✓) the correct answers.

John

1. The camp is for
   ☐ a. inner-city kids.
   ☐ b. international students.

2. At the camp, the children can
   ☐ a. take computer and math classes.
   ☐ b. play sports and enjoy the outdoors.

3. John is going to work at the camp
   ☐ a. for a week.
   ☐ b. for three or four weeks.

Maria

1. Maria is going to have an internship
   ☐ a. with a modeling agency.
   ☐ b. with an advertising agency.

2. She found out about the internship
   ☐ a. through a friend.
   ☐ b. on the Internet.

3. She will work at the agency
   ☐ a. for part of each day.
   ☐ b. for the whole day.

C ▶ Listen again. What is the best thing about each plan? Complete the sentences.

1. John will get _____ .
2. Maria will get _____ .

D *Pair work* Which plan do you think is more interesting? Give reasons for your choice.

NOISY NEIGHBORS

A *Pair work* Imagine you live below this family. Make a list of possible complaints.

B ▶ Listen to the conversations. Check (✓) the people's complaints.

1. Mrs. Rivera is complaining about
   ☐ a. loud music.
   ☐ b. strange sounds.
   ☐ c. loud voices.

2. Mr. Green is complaining because
   ☐ a. Mr. Roberti's dog chased his cat.
   ☐ b. Mike Roberti's friends use his driveway.
   ☐ c. Mike Roberti's band make too much noise.

C ▶ Listen again. How do the people solve the problems? Complete the sentences.

1. Mrs. Lang will tell her daughter to _____.

2. Mr. Roberti will tell his son's friends to _____.

D *Pair work* Role play a conversation. Use the possible complaints from part A. Take turns complaining and apologizing.

© Cambridge University Press   Photocopiable

WHAT'S THIS FOR?

A *Pair work* Look at the pictures. What do you think each gadget is used for? How do you think you use it? Compare ideas.

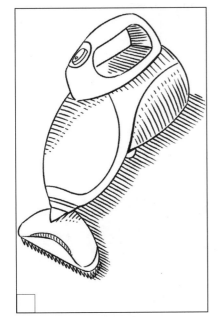

mini-vacuum

slow cooker

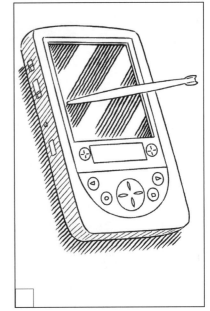

electronic address book

B ▶ Listen to people talk about the gadgets. Number the pictures from 1 to 3.

C ▶ Listen again. Check (✓) True (T) or False (F).

1.	T	F
1. It runs for 50 minutes when fully charged.	☐	☐
2. It's not necessary to change the bag very often.	☐	☐
3. You have to put it back on the charger after using it.	☐	☐

2.	T	F
1. You have to type information into it.	☐	☐
2. It can read messy handwriting.	☐	☐
3. It holds up to two thousand names and addresses.	☐	☐

3.	T	F
1. It cooks a variety of foods.	☐	☐
2. You can program it to turn on and off.	☐	☐
3. It doesn't need any liquid to cook.	☐	☐

D *Pair work* Which items in part A do you need? Which do you want? Which do you not want? Give reasons for your choices.

PARTY TIME!

A *Pair work* Look at the pictures. What do you think the people are celebrating? Compare ideas.

B ▶ Listen to people talk about different celebrations. Number the pictures from 1 to 3.

C ▶ Listen again. Complete the chart.

	What are they celebrating?	Who celebrates together?	What do they do?
1.			
2.			
3.			

D *Group work* Plan a celebration for one of these events.

birthday party   college graduation

wedding anniversary   New Year's Eve

                      Photocopiable

FUTURE PLANS

A *Pair work* The man is trying to decide what to do this summer. Look at the picture. What do you think his choices are?

B ▶ Listen to four people talk about possible plans for the summer. Check (✓) the plans they are considering.

Stan
☐ a. going waterskiing
☐ b. taking a computer course

Tammy
☐ a. going to a gym regularly
☐ b. taking cooking lessons

Janet
☐ a. taking dancing lessons
☐ b. taking a Spanish course

Stuart
☐ a. getting married
☐ b. getting a bigger apartment

C ▶ Listen again. What are the negative consequences of each plan? Complete the sentences.

1. If Stan does this, he won't be able to _____.
2. If Janet does this, she won't be able to _____.
3. If Tammy does this, she'll have to _____.
4. If Stuart does this, he'll have to _____.

D *Pair work* Write a positive consequence for each plan in part B. Then decide what you would do. Give reasons for your choices.

THE RIGHT JOB

A *Pair work* Complete the questionnaire. Then compare your answers.

Employment Questionnaire

1. What job interests you? _____

2. Why would you be good at this job? _____

3. Why do you think you'd like this job? _____

4. What do you think you might not like about this job? _____

B ⏵ Listen to people talk about the answers from their questionnaires.
Check (✓) the jobs they are describing.

1. ☐ a. flower shop clerk
   ☐ b. social worker

2. ☐ a. freelance writer
   ☐ b. TV actor

3. ☐ a. art gallery manager
   ☐ b. Web site designer

4. ☐ a. nurse
   ☐ b. computer programmer

C ⏵ Listen again. What is the problem with each job? Complete the sentences.

1. The job can be _____.

2. It's very difficult to _____.

3. This job has become _____.

4. This person would have to _____.

D *Pair work* Role play a job interview. Use the questions and answers from
the questionnaire in part A.

© Cambridge University Press   **Photocopiable**

PLACES TO SEE

A *Group work* What makes these places special or interesting? Make a list of their features.

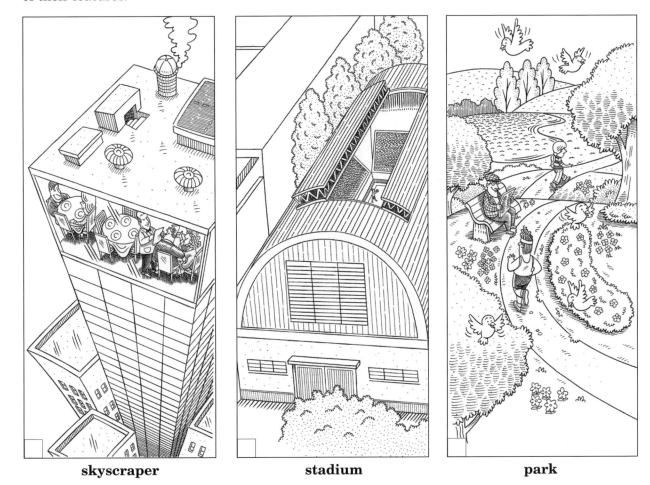

| skyscraper | stadium | park |

B ▶ Listen to a tour guide talk about the places. Number the pictures from 1 to 3.

C ▶ Listen again. Complete the sentences.

1. The place was opened _____ years ago. It's a good place to _____,
   _____, _____, and _____ .

2. This place was finished _____ years ago. It's over _____ stories
   high. There's a _____ at the top. On a clear day, you can see
   for _____ kilometers.

3. This place was opened _____ years ago. It was built for _____ and
   _____ teams. It can hold over _____ people.

D *Group work* Choose four special or interesting places in your city or town.
Write three features of each place. Present your ideas to the class.

SUCCESS STORIES

A *Pair work* Look at the cartoon strip about a man's success story.
What do you think happened? Compare ideas.

B ▶ Listen to three interviews with successful people.
Check (✓) the correct information.

1. ☐ a. The man sold a lot of paintings in his first year.
   ☐ b. He sent his work to a gallery in Los Angeles.
   ☐ c. He is well-known all over the United States.

2. ☐ a. The woman came from a musical family.
   ☐ b. She joined a Broadway show while in college.
   ☐ c. She recorded her first album last year.

3. ☐ a. The man's parents are restaurant owners.
   ☐ b. He started out selling lunches to students.
   ☐ c. He now has a different kind of business.

C ▶ Listen again. Complete the sentences.

1. The man got a lucky break when _____.

2. The woman sang the lead role when _____.

3. After the man sold his business, he _____.

D *Group work* Discuss these questions.

1. Have most successful people had lucky breaks?

2. Can you make your own luck? Is so, how?

3. Which is more important for success — hard work or a lucky break?

LET'S RENT A MOVIE!

A *Pair work* Choose three categories from the list. Then recommend a movie for each one.

B ▶ Listen to three conversations about movies.
Check (✓) True (T) or False (F).

	T	F
1.		
1. The story takes place on a train.	☐	☐
2. Some of the passengers get killed.	☐	☐
3. The man's not sure who the murderer is.	☐	☐
2.	**T**	**F**
1. The movie is about a group of people who sailed around the world.	☐	☐
2. It's a true story.	☐	☐
3. The voyage took nearly three months.	☐	☐
3.	**T**	**F**
1. The movie is an adventure story.	☐	☐
2. It's the actor's best movie.	☐	☐
3. It's about two people who have unhappy lives.	☐	☐

C ▶ Listen again. Check (✓) the word that best describes each movie.

1. ☐ silly   2. ☐ terrible   3. ☐ exciting
   ☐ suspenseful   ☐ interesting   ☐ disappointing
   ☐ boring   ☐ amusing   ☐ challenging

D *Pair work* Describe a movie you recommended in part A. Then try to persuade your partner to rent it.

DID YOU SEE THAT?

A *Pair work* Look at these gestures. What do you think each gesture means? Are any of them considered impolite in your country?

B ▶ Listen to conversations about the gestures. Number the pictures from 1 to 3.

C ▶ Listen again. Check (✓) True (T) or False (F).

1.	T	F
1. Jason was in Buenos Aires on business.	☐	☐
2. Mr. Gomez thought Jason was crazy.	☐	☐
3. The phone call was for Jason.	☐	☐

2.	T	F
1. Mrs. Johnson was trying to hurt the girl.	☐	☐
2. Mrs. Johnson has no children of her own.	☐	☐
3. Mrs. Johnson's action was not polite there.	☐	☐

3.	T	F
1. The woman thinks Don is strange.	☐	☐
2. Don is trying to help the man.	☐	☐
3. The man is nervous about singing a solo.	☐	☐

D *Group work* Write a list of "do and don't" gestures for visitors to your country. Then compare your list with the class.

© Cambridge University Press   `Photocopiable`

WHAT WOULD YOU DO?

A *Pair work* What's happening in the picture? How do you feel about it?

B ⊳ Listen to three people talk about different situations. Check (✓) the two words that best describe each person's feelings.

1. ☐ concerned
   ☐ frightened
   ☐ pleased
   ☐ disgusted

2. ☐ puzzled
   ☐ amused
   ☐ worried
   ☐ delighted

3. ☐ surprised
   ☐ embarrassed
   ☐ amused
   ☐ fascinated

C ⊳ Listen again. Check (✓) what each person probably did next.

1. ☐ a. She left the puppy there.
   ☐ b. She took the puppy home.

2. ☐ a. He called the police.
   ☐ b. He invited the man to his home.

3. ☐ a. She forgot about it.
   ☐ b. She called the friend to apologize.

D *Group work* Look at the picture in part A again. Discuss these questions.

1. What would you do if you saw this happen?

2. What would your teacher do?

3. What would you do if you were the boy? the girl?

Photocopiable

WHAT'S YOUR EXCUSE?

A *Pair work* The man is inviting the woman to dinner, but she's not interested. What excuse did she make? Think of two more excuses for her to use.

B ▶ Listen to four invitations. Complete the chart.

	Event	When	Where
1.			
2.			
3.			
4.			

C ▶ Listen again. Check (✓) whether the people accept or refuse. If they refuse, write the excuse.

	Accept	Refuse	Excuse
1.	☐	☐	
2.	☐	☐	
3.	☐	☐	
4.	☐	☐	

D *Pair work* Role play the conversation in part A.

© Cambridge University Press

1 FROM MEXICO TO BRAZIL

Complete these questions.

1. _____ Alex born?

   He was born in Mexico.

2. _____ he move to Brazil?

   When he was five years old.

3. _____ brothers born in Mexico?

   No, they weren't. They were born in Brazil.

4. _____ grow up?

   They grew up in Salvador.

5. _____ to college in Salvador?

   No, he didn't. He went to college in São Paulo.

6. _____ study?

   He studied law.

Alex Martinez

2 WHEN YOU WERE YOUNGER . . .

A Add three questions to the survey. Then check (✓) Yes or No.

When you were younger . . .	Yes	No
1. did you use to eat a lot of snacks?	☐	☐
2. did you use to have a pet?	☐	☐
3. did you use to watch a lot of TV?	☐	☐
4. did you use to collect anything?	☐	☐
5. did you use to ?	☐	☐
6. did you use to ?	☐	☐
7. did you use to ?	☐	☐

B *Pair work* Ask and answer the questions from part A. Add follow-up questions.

A: When you were younger, did you use to eat a lot of snacks?

B: Yes, I did.

A: What kind of snacks did you use to eat?

① STREET INTERVIEW

Complete the conversation.

Reporter: Do you think New York City is a better place to live than in the past?

Maria: In general, yes it is. There is ___*less*___ (fewer / less) pollution these days. There is _____ (fewer / less) crime, too, but we still need _____ (more / much) police officers.

Reporter: And what other things need to be improved?

Maria: Well, there isn't _____ (enough / more) good public transportation, so there are too _____ (many / much) cars on the streets. There's always too _____ (many / much) traffic downtown, and there aren't _____ (fewer / enough) parking spaces.

Reporter: Thank you for your views.

② THE TOURIST

Pair work Role play conversations between a tourist and a resident of your city or town. Ask about the location, opening hours, and closing times for the places in the box.

bank	drugstore	library	shopping mall
coffee shop	laundromat	post office	supermarket

A: Excuse me. Can you tell me where the shopping mall is?

B: The shopping mall? It's across the street from the park.

A: And when does it open?

B: Let me see . . .

1 MOVING HOUSES

Complete this e-mail. Use *not . . . enough*, *too*, or *not as . . . as* and the adjectives in parentheses.

September 4

Dear Fred,

I moved into my new apartment yesterday, and it's really nice. It's very large, so it's ___not as cramped as___ (cramped) the old one. My old place was ________________ (big) for me. And more important, it's brighter. My old place was ________________ (dark). Unfortunately, the neighborhood is ________________ (convenient) my old one. There are ________________ buses and there's no subway nearby, so I drive to work. Shopping is also more difficult. The stores are really nice, but they're ________________ (expensive) for me! I hope you can come and see it soon.

Love,
Sylvia

2 THE WISH GAME

A ***Group work*** Imagine you are the people in these pictures. Write as many *I wish* sentences for each person as possible.

	Picture 1
	1. I wish I didn't have so much homework.
	2. I wish I could play with my friends.

B ***Group work*** Read your sentences to the class. Which group has the most sentences?

© Cambridge University Press **Photocopiable**

1 A PIZZA RECIPE

A Put the words in order to make sentences.

[5] cheese / after that / the sauce / cover / with

After that, cover the sauce with cheese.

☐ the dough / bake / then / for five minutes

_____

☐ the oven / the dough / take / out of / after that

_____

☐ over the dough / tomato sauce / spread / next

_____

☐ roll out / the dough / into a circle / first

_____

☐ the pizza / in a preheated oven / bake / until / the cheese melts / finally

_____

B Number the sentences from 1 to 6 to make a recipe.

2 FOOD EXPERIENCES

A Complete questions 1 to 3.

1. Have you ever eaten _____ ? (an usual food)

2. Have you ever been to _____ ? (name of a restaurant)

3. Have you ever made _____ ? (a dish)

4. Have you ever had a really good meal?

5. Have you ever had a really bad meal?

B *Group work* Ask and answer the questions from part A. Add follow-up questions.

A: Have you ever eaten ceviche?

B: No, I haven't. But I've eaten snake.

C: Really? When did you eat it?

B: Last summer . . .

© Cambridge University Press   **Photocopiable**

1 SUNDAY PLANS

Complete the conversation with the correct form of *be going to* or *will*.

A: What ___*are you going to*___ do on Saturday?

B: I _____ take some friends for a drive. There's a beautiful

   national park not far from here.

A: That sounds great. But you don't have a car.

B: I guess we _____ rent a camper.

A: _____ you _____ come back on

   the same day?

B: I'm not sure. Maybe we _____ stay there for one

   night and come back on Sunday. It _____ be lots of fun!

   We _____ probably go sailing if the weather's nice.

A: Really? I love sailing!

B: Say, would you like to come with us?

A: Thanks, but I think I _____ stay home this weekend.

   It's my sister's birthday.

2 WHAT SHOULD I DO?

Group work Read these problems and ask for advice. Take turns.

1. I need to lose weight, but chocolate is my favorite food.

2. I'm moving to Mexico, but I can't speak any Spanish.

3. I invited my mother-in-law for dinner, and I am a terrible cook!

4. I missed three classes last week, and there's a test tomorrow.

5. I've lost my friend's book, and now he wants it back.

6. I've had a terrible headache for several days.

7. I forgot to call my best friend on her birthday.

8. I have trouble getting up early in the morning, so I'm always late for work.

A: I need to lose weight, but chocolate is my favorite food.

B: You don't have to give up chocolate. But you should eat more fruit.

C: And you have to exercise more . . .

1 REQUESTS

Complete the requests with the correct word in parentheses.

1. Turn _____ *down* _____ (down / up / on) the radio. I'm trying to study.

2. Turn _____ (down / off / on) the television. I'd like to watch the news.

3. Hang _____ (over / down / up) your clothes. They're on the floor.

4. Take the dog _____ (away / out / off) for a walk. He needs to exercise.

5. Clean _____ (up / away / off) your room. It's a mess!

6. Pick _____ (up / down / over) the newspaper. It's on the floor.

7. Take _____ (in / out / off) the garbage. The trashcan is full.

8. Take _____ (away / out / off) your coat. It's warm in here.

9. Put _____ (away / off / on) the groceries. They're in the kitchen.

10. Turn _____ (on / off / out) the lights. I can't see a thing!

2 RESPONDING TO REQUESTS

Pair work Make conversations using the requests from Exercise 1 and
the expressions in the box. Your partner responds.

Can you . . . ?
Could you . . . ?
Would you please . . . ?
Would you mind . . . ?

A: Could you turn down the radio?
   I'm trying to study.

B: Of course. I didn't realize it was
   so loud.

© Cambridge University Press   Photocopiable

① COMPUTER TECHNOLOGY

Complete the sentences with the correct form of *be used to* or *be used for*.

1. Credit cards _____*are used to*_____ buy things on the Internet.
2. Computers _____ sending and receiving e-mails.
3. The Internet _____ downloading music.
4. System software _____ run the hardware in a computer.
5. Application software _____ doing specific tasks on a computer.
6. CD-ROMs _____ storing information.
7. Webcams _____ take photos and post them on the World Wide Web.
8. Scanners _____ change photographs into digital images.
9. A mouse _____ move the pointer on a computer screen.
10. A keyboard _____ typing information on a computer.

② GUESSING GAME

A Choose one item from the box. Write four pieces of advice for using it.
Don't write the name of the item.

answering machine	DVD player
camcorder	electronic address book
cell phone	electronic dictionary
computer	printer
CD player	television

> *Don't forget to recharge the battery.*
> *Remember to put a tape in it.*

B *Group work* Read your advice. Your classmates guess the items.

A: Don't forget to recharge the battery.

B: Is it a cell phone?

A: No, it isn't. Remember to put a tape in it.

C: Is it a camcorder?

A: That's right.

SPECIAL DAYS

Put the words in order to make sentences.

1. when / Americans / the day / July 4 / Independence / is / celebrate
   July 4 is the day when Americans celebrate Independence.

2. when / change colors / is / the season / some trees / fall
   _____

3. many people / the beach / summer / is / go to / when / a time of year
   _____

4. when / a bride and groom / is / a time / go on vacation together / a honeymoon
   _____

5. northern hemisphere / when / spring begins / is the month / in the / March
   _____

6. New Year's resolutions / January 1 / make / the day / is / when some people
   _____

2 **QUIZ**

A Write six sentences about a celebration. Use the words *before*, *when*, and *after*.
Do not write the name of the celebration.

	Before we go to the ceremony, we put on caps and gowns.
	When we walk onto the stage, we get our diplomas.
	After we get our diplomas, a photographer takes our picture.

B *Pair work* Rewrite the sentences without the words *before*, *when*, and *after*.
Then exchange papers. Complete the sentences and guess the celebration.

_____	*we go to the ceremony, we put on caps and gowns.*
_____	*we walk onto the stage, we get our diplomas.*
_____	*we get our diplomas, a photographer takes our picture.*

A: Is it a graduation ceremony?

B: That's right.

© Cambridge University Press   **Photocopiable**

① WHAT WILL HAPPEN?

Complete the sentences with your own information.

1. If I win a lot of money, _____

   _____

2. If I lose my job, _____

   _____

3. If I have more free time next year, _____

   _____

4. If I exercise more, _____

   _____

5. If _____, I'll have to move.

6. If _____, I might buy a new car.

7. If _____, I'll be very surprised.

8. If _____, I'll be very happy.

② OUR CHANGING WORLD

A How were these things in the past? How are they now? How will they be in the future? Complete the chart with your ideas.

Topic	Past	Present	Future
Shopping	small stores	large malls	on-line shopping
Communication		cell phones	
Transportation		cars, trains, planes	

B *Group work* Compare your ideas.

A: In the past, there were no large malls. There were only small stores.

B: That's right. Now most people shop at malls. What about the future?

C: In the future, I think people will buy everything on the Internet.

1 HOW ABOUT YOU?

Write responses to agree and disagree with the statements. Use expressions from the box.

So do I.	Neither do I.	Really? I like it.	Oh, I don't mind.
So am I.	Neither am I.	Oh, I don't.	Well, I do.
I am!	Neither can I.	Gee, I'm not.	

Statements	Agree	Disagree
1. I really like playing tennis.	*So do I.*	*Oh, I don't.*
2. I don't mind riding the bus.		
3. I can't stand driving in traffic.		
4. I'm interested in jazz.		
5. I'm very good at drawing.		
6. I'm not good at dancing.		

2 THE BEST CANDIDATE

A Read the job description and statements from three candidates. Rank the candidates from 1 (first choice) to 3 (third choice).

> ### Sales Manager, Latin America
>
> Must have five years' sales management experience and strong communication, computer, and presentation skills. Must speak English and Spanish fluently and be able to travel. Prefer business degree. Knowledge of Portuguese a plus.

☐ "I have a degree in computer science and six years' management experience. I grew up in Chicago, and I studied a little Spanish and Portuguese in high school. I don't like to give presentations, but I love to travel. I spent two weeks in South America, and I loved it!"

☐ "I have an MBA in Finance, five years' management experience, and strong computer skills. I love to give presentations, and I'm free to travel. My native language is Spanish, and I speak English fluently. I don't know any Portuguese, but I'm willing to learn."

☐ "I speak English and Spanish fluently, but Portuguese is my mother tongue. I have a business degree and four years' management experience. I've also worked in Latin America, and I've given many presentations there. I'm able to travel one week a month."

B *Group work* Compare your choices and give reasons for them.

DID YOU KNOW . . . ?

Change these active sentences into the passive.

1. The Greeks built the Parthenon in the fifth century B.C.

   The Parthenon was built by the Greeks in the fifth century B.C.

2. Russia sold Alaska to the United States in the 1860s.

   _____

3. Egyptian workers constructed the Suez Canal in the 1860s.

   _____

4. The U.S. government created Yellowstone Park in 1872.

   _____

5. French architect Gustave Eiffel designed the Eiffel Tower.

   _____

2 CURRENCIES AND LANGUAGES

A What do you know about world currencies and languages?
Match the countries with the currencies and languages.

Currencies	Countries	Official languages
bolívar	1. Argentina	Afrikaans
dollar	2. Brazil	English
guaraní	3. Japan	Japanese
peso	4. Korea	Korean
rand	5. Mexico	Mandarin Chinese
real	6. Paraguay	Portuguese
sol	7. Peru	Spanish
won	8. South Africa	
yen	9. Taiwan	
	10. Venezuela	

B *Pair work* Compare your answers.

A: I think the bolívar is used in Venezuela.

B: And what language is spoken there?

A: Is it Spanish?

B: I think so.

Check your answers:

1. peso, Spanish 2. real, Portuguese 3. yen, Japanese 4. won, Korean 5. peso, Spanish 6. guaraní, Spanish 7. sol, Spanish 8. rand, Afrikaans and English 9. dollar, Mandarin Chinese 10. bolívar, Spanish

1 UNFORGETTABLE MOMENTS

Complete these sentences with the appropriate form of the verbs in parentheses.

1. We _____ (have) a wonderful surprise a
   month after we _____ (get) married. One
   night while we _____ (cook) dinner, we
   _____ (hear) a strange noise outside.
   When we _____ (open) the door, we
   _____ (find) a puppy!

2. My husband and I _____ (ice-skate) when
   we _____ (meet). I _____
   (fall) down because I _____ (look) at him.
   It was really embarrassing!

3. Last summer, we _____ (see) a tornado
   while we _____ (travel) in the U.S.
   It was really scary!

4. Last weekend, we _____ (watch) TV when
   the phone _____ (ring). It was my best friend
   from high school!

2 WHAT HAVE YOU BEEN DOING LATELY?

A *Group work* Write five questions using the present perfect continuous on a
piece of paper.

How have you been feeling lately?
Have you been going to the gym much recently?

B *Group work* Exchange questions with another group. Take turns
asking and answering the questions.

© Cambridge University Press   Photocopiable

1 HOW DID YOU LIKE IT?

Complete the conversation with the correct word in parentheses.

Mike: What did you think of the movie, Linda?

Linda: I'm afraid I thought it was _____boring_____ (bored / boring).

Mike: Really? I thought the special effects were _____ (fascinated / fascinating).

Linda: They were pretty _____ (interested / interesting), I suppose. But I preferred the book.

Mike: I was _____ (surprised / surprising) that the book and the movie were so similar.

Linda: What did you think of the book?

Mike: I really liked it. I thought it was _____ (amazed / amazing).

2 YOUR FAVORITES

A What kind of magazines, books, TV programs, and movies do you like? What kind don't you like? Complete the chart.

	Like	Don't like
Magazines		
Books		
TV programs		
Movies		

B *Group work* Talk about your likes and dislikes.

A: I like magazines that have lots of interesting photos. I don't like magazines that have a lot of words.

B: I prefer magazines that have information about celebrities.

C: Really? I like magazines that . . .

1 MAY I?

A Complete the chart with the words in the box.

| are allowed to | can | have to |
| aren't allowed to | can't | have got to |

Permission	Obligation	Prohibition

B Write each sentence a different way.

1. You can ride your bike here.   _You're allowed to ride your bike here._

2. You aren't allowed to park your car here.   _____

3. You're allowed to camp here.   _____

4. You have to wear shoes.   _____

5. You've got to wear your seat belt.   _____

6. You can't chew gum in class.   _____

2 STRANGE HAPPENINGS

Group work Imagine you are in these situations. What do you think they mean? Compare your ideas.

1. You walk into your classroom. There are no people there.

2. You are driving a car. A police officer stops you.

3. It's 3:00 A.M. You hear a loud noise outside your door.

4. You receive a greeting card. There is no message and no return address.

5. You find an old portrait in your garage. The person looks like you.

A: You walk into your classroom. There are no people there.
   What do you think it means?

B: It might mean you're in the wrong classroom.

C: Or maybe you're very, very late for class!

© Cambridge University Press

1 WHAT WOULD YOU DO?

What would you do in these situations? Complete the sentences.

1. A classmate wants to copy your homework.

   If that happened to me, I _would say, "No way!"_____

2. I forgot my key, and I can't get into my apartment.

   If I couldn't get into my apartment, I _____

3. I just finished an expensive meal, and I can't find my wallet.

   If I were in that situation, I _____

4. A friend always calls me late at night, when I'm trying to sleep.

   If a friend did that to me, I'd _____

2 WHAT WOULD YOU HAVE DONE?

Group work What would you have done in these situations? Compare your ideas.

1. A friend from Australia stayed with me for a month.
   After she left, I got a $500 phone bill, and all the
   international calls were to Australia! My friend said
   she didn't make the calls, so I paid the bill.

2. My cousin plans to marry his girlfriend, but I really
   don't like her. My cousin asked me for my opinion
   about the marriage. I lied and said I was very happy
   about it.

3. A friend said something that I didn't agree with. I told
   her she was wrong. She was very angry, and now
   she isn't talking to me.

4. I forgot about my best friend's birthday party.
   I didn't call him to apologize, though.
   I was too embarrassed.

A: If a friend did that to me, I wouldn't have paid the bill.

B: I would have called a lawyer!

C: I would have told all her friends about it!

① DON'T FORGET TO . . .

A teacher made these requests. Rewrite the requests using the words in parentheses.

1. Read the article on page 103. (tell)

   The teacher told us to read the article on page 103.

2. Study the new words in the article. (say)

   _____

3. Don't look up every new word in the dictionary. (ask)

   _____

4. Can you bring a newspaper to class? (ask)

   _____

5. Don't read the newspaper before class. (say)

   _____

6. Don't be late for class. (tell)

   _____

② WHAT AN EXCUSE!

A Imagine you didn't listen to the teacher's requests in part A. Write an excuse for each request. (Use your imagination.)

1. My dog ate the article.

2. I lost my glasses.

B *Class activity* Exchange papers with a partner. Then tell the class your partner's excuses.

"Pedro said he didn't read the article because his dog ate it . . ."

1 YOUR VOCABULARY LOG

Make a vocabulary log. Write words or draw pictures to help you remember.

~ CHILDHOOD MEMORIES ~

beach	_____	*Pl*
bicycle	_____	___
bird	_____	___
cat	_____	___
chess	_____	___
childhood	_____	___
collect	_____	___
comics	_____	___
doll	_____	___
farm	_____	___
hobby	_____	___
lesson	_____	___

nickname	_____	___
memory	_____	___
paint	_____	___
rabbit	_____	___
scrapbook	_____	___
shell	_____	___
snake	_____	___
soccer ball	_____	___
summer camp	_____	___
teddy bear	_____	___
tree house	_____	___
trumpet	_____	___

(*italics* = new word)

2 PRACTICE

A Classify the words in your vocabulary log. Write **G** for *games*, **Pl** for *places*, **Po** for *possessions*, **Pt** for *pets*, or **O** for *other*.

B Write five sentences about your childhood. Use at least five words from your vocabulary log.

> *When I was a child, I used to collect dolls.*

Then rewrite your sentences on another piece of paper. Omit the words from your vocabulary log.

> *When I was a child, I used to* _____ _____ .

C *Pair work* Exchange papers and complete the sentences. Then read them aloud. How many are correct?

① YOUR VOCABULARY LOG

Make a vocabulary log. Write words or draw pictures to help you remember.

COMPOUND NOUNS

bicycle lane	_____ ○	stop sign	_____ ____
bus schedule	_____ ____	street light	_____ ____
bus station	_____ ____	subway line	_____ ____
bus stop	_____ ____	subway station	_____ ____
firefighter	_____ ____	subway stop	_____ ____
fire station	_____ ____	*taxi driver*	_____ ____
fire truck	_____ ____	taxi stand	_____ ____
newsstand	_____ ____	traffic jam	_____ ____
parking garage	_____ ____	traffic light	_____ ____
parking space	_____ ____	*train schedule*	_____ ____
police car	_____ ____	train station	_____ ____
police officer	_____ ____	train stop	_____ ____
police station	_____ ____		

(*italics* = new word)

② PRACTICE

A Classify the words in your vocabulary log. Write **C** for *cars*, **Pe** for *people*,
Pl for *places*, **S** for *signs and lights*, or **O** for *other*.

B Write clues for five words from your vocabulary log.

1. *You can ride your bike there.*   4. _____

2. _____   5. _____

3. _____   6. _____

C *Pair work* Read your clues aloud. Your partner guesses. Take turns.

A: You can ride your bike there.

B: Is it a bicycle lane?

A: That's right.

① YOUR VOCABULARY LOG

Make a vocabulary log. Write words or draw pictures to help you remember.

HOUSES AND APARTMENTS

bright	_____ ___	
comfortable	_____ ___	
convenient	_____ ___	
cramped	_____ ___	
dangerous	_____ ___	
dark	_____ ___	
dingy	_____ ___	
expensive	_____ ___	
huge	_____ ___	
inconvenient	_____ ___	
modern	_____ ___	

neat	_____ ___	
noisy	_____ ___	
private	_____ ___	
quiet	_____ ___	
safe	_____ ___	
shabby	_____ ___	
small	_____ ___	
spacious	_____ ___	
tiny	_____ ___	
uncomfortable	_____ ___	
untidy	_____ ___	

(*italics* = new word)

② PRACTICE

A Classify the words in your vocabulary log. Write **+** for *positive words*,
– for *negative words*, or **O** for *neutral words*.

B Write nine pairs of antonyms. Use words from your vocabulary log and
other words you know.

1. *bright ≠ dark* _____
2. _____
3. _____
4. _____
5. _____

6. _____
7. _____
8. _____
9. _____
10. _____

C *Pair work* Write a short description of your classroom. Use at least
five words from your vocabulary log. Then share it with the class.

© Cambridge University Press   **Photocopiable**   *Vocabulary Log: Unit 3* • 35

1 YOUR VOCABULARY LOG

Make a vocabulary log. Write words or draw pictures to help you remember.

• COOKING •

appetizer	_____	F	fish	_____	____
bagel	_____	____	fry	_____	
bake	_____	____	guacamole dip	_____	
banana	_____		menu	_____	
barbecue	_____		onion	_____	
beef	_____		peanut butter	_____	
boil	_____	____	popcorn	_____	
chicken	_____	____	potato	_____	
diet	_____		recipe	_____	
dish	_____	____	roast	_____	
egg	_____		shrimp	_____	
eggplant	_____	____	steam	_____	

2 PRACTICE

A Classify the words in your vocabulary log. Write **C** for *cooking methods*, **F** for *foods*, or **O** for *other*.

B Complete the chart with popular foods and cooking methods in your country.

	Popular foods	Popular cooking methods
1.	*potatoes*	*boiling, frying*
2.		
3.		
4.		

C *Group work* Share the foods and cooking methods from your chart. How many are similar? How many are different?

© Cambridge University Press Photocopiable

1 *YOUR VOCABULARY LOG*

Make a vocabulary log. Write words or draw pictures to help you remember.

TRAVEL PLANNING

backpack	_____	_E_	overnight bag	_____ _____
camper	_____ _____		pack	_____ _____
camping	_____ _____		passport	_____ _____
cash	_____ _____		plane ticket	_____ _____
credit card	_____ _____		round-trip	_____ _____
first-aid kit	_____ _____		shorts	_____ _____
fishing rod	_____ _____		suitcase	_____ _____
hiking boots	_____ _____		*tent*	_____ _____
hotel reservation	_____ _____		traveler's check	_____ _____
identification	_____ _____		vaccination	_____ _____
medication	_____ _____		visa	_____ _____
national park	_____ _____		windbreaker	_____ _____

(*italics* = new word)

2 *PRACTICE*

A Classify the words in your vocabulary log. Write **C** for *clothes*, **D** for *documents*, **E** for *equipment*, **M** for *money*, or **O** for *other*.

B Make a list of four things for each category. Include one that doesn't belong.

Camping trip	Business trip	Fishing trip	Beach vacation
tent			
~~hotel reservation~~			
backpack			
first-aid kit			

C *Pair work* Exchange papers. Cross out the things that don't belong. Then check your answers.

YOUR VOCABULARY LOG

Make a vocabulary log. Write words or draw pictures to help you remember.

AT HOME			
clean up	_2V_	put away	
garbage		stereo	
groceries		take off	
hang up		take out	
laptop		throw out	
let out		towels	
mess		trash	
microwave		turn down	
newspaper		turn off	
pick up		turn on	

2 PRACTICE

A Classify the words in your vocabulary log. Write **2V** for *two-part verbs* or **O** for *other*.

B Add a word or phrase to these two-part verbs from your vocabulary log.

1. clean ___this mess___ up
2. hang _____ up
3. let _____ out
4. pick _____ up
5. put _____ away
6. take _____ out
7. throw _____ out
8. turn _____ down
9. turn _____ off
10. turn _____ on

C Imagine you are having a party. Make a list of things to do before and after the party. Use words from your vocabulary log.

	Before the party	After the party
1.	Pick up the groceries	
2.		
3.		
4.		

© Cambridge University Press   Photocopiable

1 YOUR VOCABULARY LOG

Make a vocabulary log. Write words or draw pictures to help you remember.

COMPUTERS AND THEIR USES

battery	_____ N	menu	_____ ____
browse	_____ ____	monitor	_____ ____
CD-ROM	_____ ____	mouse	_____ ____
cut and paste	_____ ____	photographs	_____ ____
disk drive	_____ ____	recharge	_____ ____
document	_____ ____	*save*	_____ ____
double-click (on)	_____ ____	*scan*	_____ ____
drag and drop	_____ ____	screen	_____ ____
format	_____ ____	store	_____ ____
highlight	_____ ____	surf	_____ ____
icon	_____ ____	text	_____ ____
information	_____ ____	the net	_____ ____
keyboard	_____ ____	Web sites	_____ ____

(*italics* = new word)

2 PRACTICE

A Classify the words in your vocabulary log. Write **N** for *nouns* or **V** for *verbs*.

B Write five things you can do with a computer. Use words from your vocabulary log.

1. *scan photographs* _____
2. _____
3. _____
4. _____
5. _____
6. _____

C *Pair work* Write a description of your dream computer. What will it do?
Use words from your vocabulary log. Then read your description to the class.

> *Our dream computer will save money and time. It won't need a disk drive
> or a mouse . . .*

① YOUR VOCABULARY LOG

Make a vocabulary log. Write words or draw pictures to help you remember.

CELEBRATIONS

anniversary	_____	C	newlywed	_____	___
bride	_____	___	New Year's Eve	_____	___
ceremony	_____	___	occasion	_____	___
date	_____	___	parade	_____	___
dress up	_____	___	party	_____	___
engagement	_____	___	reception	_____	___
fireworks	_____	___	resolution	_____	___
fruit punch	_____	___	speech	_____	___
gift	_____	___	Thanksgiving	_____	___
groom	_____	___	Valentine's Day	_____	___
honeymoon	_____	___	wedding	_____	___
Mother's Day	_____	___			

② PRACTICE

A Classify the words in your vocabulary log. Write **C** for *celebrations*, **P** for *people*, **T** for *things*, or **O** for *other*.

B Think of a special celebration. Complete the chart. Use words from your vocabulary log.

Celebration	
Date	
Foods	
Activities	
Things you gave or received	

C *Pair work* Tell your partner about the celebration in part B.

© Cambridge University Press

1 YOUR VOCABULARY LOG

Make a vocabulary log. Write words or draw pictures to help you remember.

>>>>>>>>>>>>>>>>>> EVENTS AND CONSEQUENCES <<<<<<<<<<<<<<<<<<

buy a large dog	_____ ___	get requests for loans	_____ ___
buy expensive clothes	_____ ___	give up your favorite snack	_____ ___
fall in love	_____ ___	go on a diet	_____ ___
fall out of love	_____ ___	have a lot more free time	_____ ___
feel better about yourself	_____ ___	inherit a lot of money	_____ ___
feel hungry a lot	_____ ___	learn a new language	_____ ___
feel jealous	_____ ___	lose touch with old friends	_____ ___
feel more tired	_____ ___	move to a foreign country	_____ ___
feel safer in your home	_____ ___	*start a new job*	_____ ___
feel worse about yourself	_____ ___	*stop studying*	_____ ___

(*italics* = new phrase)

2 PRACTICE

A Classify the phrases in your vocabulary log. Write **+** for *positive phrases*, **–** for *negative phrases*, or **O** for *neutral phrases*.

B Write five sentences about events and consequences. Use phrases from your vocabulary log.

	If I go on a diet, I'll be hungry a lot.

Then write each event and consequence on separate pieces of paper.

	I go on a diet

	I feel hungry a lot

C *Pair work* Exchange papers. Match the events with the consequences. Then check your answers.

 Vocabulary Log: Unit 9 • **41**

1 YOUR VOCABULARY LOG

Make a vocabulary log. Write words or draw pictures to help you remember.

JOBS

accountant _____

architect _____

bookkeeper _____

doctor _____

journalist _____

lawyer _____

model _____

nurse _____

songwriter _____

stockbroker _____

teacher _____

waiter _____

PERSONALITY TRAITS

creative _____

critical _____

efficient _____

generous _____

hardworking _____

impatient _____

level-headed _____

organized _____

patient _____

punctual _____

reliable _____

strict _____

2 PRACTICE

A Classify the jobs in your vocabulary log. Write **$** for *low salary*, **$$** for *average salary*, or **$$$** for *high salary*.

B Classify the personality traits in your vocabulary log. Do these traits describe you? Write **A** for *always*, **U** for *usually*, **S** for *sometimes*, or **N** for *never*.

C *Pair work* Choose five jobs from your vocabulary log. List the three most important personality traits for each job. Then share your answers with the class.

YOUR VOCABULARY LOG

Make a vocabulary log. Write words or draw pictures to help you remember.

INDUSTRIES

cars	_____	_N_
catch	_____	___
cattle	_____	___
chickens	_____	___
coffee	_____	___
consume	_____	___
corn	_____	___
cultivate	_____	___
electronics	_____	___
employ	_____	___
export	_____	___
farm	_____	___
grow	_____	___

industry	_____	___
lobsters	_____	___
manufacture	_____	___
microchips	_____	___
oysters	_____	___
raise	_____	___
rice	_____	___
seafood	_____	___
sheep	_____	___
shrimp	_____	___
tea	_____	___
televisions	_____	___
textiles	_____	___

② PRACTICE

A Classify the words in your vocabulary log. Write **N** for *nouns* or **V** for *verbs*.

B Choose three countries. Write four clues for each country, but do not write the country's name. Use words from your vocabulary log and your own words.

manufacture electronics, grow rice, use the yen, catch and export seafood

C *Pair work* Read your clues aloud. Your partner guesses. Take turns.

A: manufacture electronics, grow rice, use the yen, catch and export seafood

B: Hmm. Is it Japan?

A: That's right.

1 YOUR VOCABULARY LOG

Make a vocabulary log. Write words or draw pictures to help you remember.

TIME EXPRESSIONS

With the simple past and past continuous:

during my childhood _____

last month _____

last year _____

last week _____

many years ago _____

two years ago _____

on my first day
of school _____

when I was in
elementary school _____

With the present perfect and present perfect continuous:

for ten years _____

for the last six months _____

for the past few months _____

lately _____

recently _____

since yesterday _____

these days _____

this year _____

(*italics* = new word)

2 PRACTICE

A Write six sentences about events in your life. Use time expressions from your vocabulary log and your own words.

During my childhood, I lived in Australia.

For three years now, I've been living in France.

Then write each event and time expression on separate pieces of paper.

During my childhood,

I lived in Australia.

For three years now,

I've been living in France.

B Exchange papers. Match the events with the time expressions. Then check your answers.

Photocopiable

YOUR VOCABULARY LOG

Make a vocabulary log. Write words or draw pictures to help you remember.

DESCRIPTIVE ADJECTIVES

absurd	_____	___	marvelous	_____	___
amazing	_____	___	odd	_____	___
awful	_____	___	outstanding	_____	___
bizarre	_____	___	ridiculous	_____	___
disgusting	_____	___	silly	_____	___
dreadful	_____	___	*strange*	_____	___
dumb	_____	___	*stupid*	_____	___
fabulous	_____	___	surprising	_____	___
fantastic	_____	___	terrible	_____	___
fascinating	_____	___	unusual	_____	___
frightening	_____	___	weird	_____	___
horrible	_____	___	wonderful	_____	___

(*italics* = new word)

PRACTICE

A Classify the words in your vocabulary log. Write **+** for *positive words* or **–** for *negative words*.

B Complete the chart. Write the names of three movies you have seen. Then write three adjectives that describe each movie. Use words from your vocabulary log.

	Movie	Adjectives		
1.				
2.				
3.				

C *Group work* Tell your classmates about the movies from part B.

1 *YOUR VOCABULARY LOG*

Make a vocabulary log. Write words or draw pictures to help you remember.

FEELINGS

amazed	_____	_F_	embarrassed	_____	_____
amazing	_____	_____	*embarrassing*	_____	_____
annoyed	_____	_____	exhausted	_____	_____
annoying	_____	_____	*exhausting*	_____	_____
bored	_____	_____	*frightened*	_____	_____
boring	_____	_____	*frightening*	_____	_____
confused	_____	_____	*revolted*	_____	_____
confusing	_____	_____	*revolting*	_____	_____
disappointed	_____	_____	frustrated	_____	_____
disappointing	_____	_____	*frustrating*	_____	_____
disgusted	_____	_____	irritated	_____	_____
disgusting	_____	_____	*irritating*	_____	_____

(*italics* = new word)

2 *PRACTICE*

A Classify the words in your vocabulary log. Write **F** for *feelings* or **T** for *things that cause feelings*.

B How do you feel in these situations? What do you say? Complete the chart. Use words from your vocabulary log.

	I feel . . .	I say, "It's . . ."
You see a snake.		
You leave your homework at home.		
You have to wait for a long time.		
You read about a very bad crime.		
You watch a horror movie.		
Something is worse than you expected.		

C *Pair work* Compare your answers from part B.

A: How do you feel when you see a snake?

B: I feel scared.

A: Really? I feel revolted.

© Cambridge University Press   **Photocopiable**

① YOUR VOCABULARY LOG

Make a vocabulary log. Write words or draw pictures to help you remember.

ANTONYMS

accept ≠ refuse	_____ D
admit ≠ deny	_____
agree ≠ disagree	_____ S
borrow ≠ lend	_____
connect ≠ disconnect	_____
fasten ≠ unfasten	_____
find ≠ lose	_____
increase ≠ decrease	_____
enjoy ≠ dislike	_____
marry ≠ divorce	_____
remember ≠ forget	_____
save ≠ spend	_____

(*italics* = new word)

② PRACTICE

A Classify the antonyms in your vocabulary log. Write **S** for *same stem* (basic part of a word) or **D** for *different stem*.

B Write five pairs of sentences using antonyms from your vocabulary log.

> *I didn't accept his invitation. I refused it.*

Then rewrite your sentences on another piece of paper. Omit the words from your vocabulary log.

> *I didn't _____ his invitation. I _____ it.*

C *Pair work* Exchange papers and complete the sentences. Then read them aloud. How many are correct?

1 YOUR VOCABULARY LOG

Make a vocabulary log. Write words or draw pictures to help you remember.

VERB AND NOUN PAIRS

express anger	_____ ___		make an apology	_____ ___
express concern	_____ ___		make an excuse	_____ ___
express *gratitude*	_____ ___		make an invitation	_____ ___
express regrets	_____ ___		make *a remark*	_____ ___
give a compliment	_____ ___		offer congratulations	_____ ___
give advice	_____ ___		offer *help*	_____ ___
give an excuse	_____ ___		offer sympathy	_____ ___
give *an explanation*	_____ ___		tell a joke	_____ ___
give a reason	_____ ___		tell a lie	_____ ___
make a complaint	_____ ___		tell *a story*	_____ ___
make a criticism	_____ ___		tell the truth	_____ ___

(*italics* = new word)

2 PRACTICE

A Classify the words in your vocabulary log. Write **E** for *easy to do* or **D** for *difficult to do*.

B What do the speakers want to do? Write words from your vocabulary log.

1. "This food is terrible! I want to talk to the manager." *make a complaint* _____

2. "Do you need some help with those bags?" _____

3. "I can't come to school. I need to go to the doctor." _____

4. "I'm really worried about you." _____

5. "I think this movie is terrible!" _____

6. "You shouldn't eat sugar. It's bad for you." _____

7. "Have you heard the one about the boy who . . . ?" _____

8. "Would you like to come to my party?" _____

C *Pair work* Write three sentences or questions that express different purposes from your vocabulary log. Then read your sentences aloud. Your partner guesses.

A: I really appreciate your help.

B: You're expressing gratitude.

A: That's right.

© Cambridge University Press   **Photocopiable**

1 BEFORE YOU WRITE

Read the new employee announcement. How does the manager organize
the information? Check (✓) the correct diagram.

September 15th

Marie Kelt

I am pleased to announce the appointment of Marie Kelt as our new translator for French and
Portuguese. Marie joined T&I services at the beginning of this week.
Marie is a native speaker of French, and she speaks Portuguese and English fluently. She got
a Bachelor of Arts degree in translation four years ago.
After that, she worked as a junior translator for a Los Angeles law firm for two years. In her
most recent position, she was a translator for an international company in New York City.
Let's all welcome Marie to T&I Services.
Linda Black
Manager

T & I
SERVICES

☐1.
- Announcement
- Welcome
- Work experience
- Education

☐2.
- Announcement
- Education
- Work experience
- Welcome

☐3.
- Announcement
- Education
- Welcome
- Work experience

2 YOUR FIRST DRAFT

A Imagine you are a manager. You just hired a new employee for a position
with your company. Complete the chart.

Name of company:	Employee's education:
Name of employee:	Employee's work experience:
Position with company:	Other qualifications:

B Write an announcement about the new employee. Use your notes and
the announcement in Exercise 1 as a model.

C *Pair work* Read your partner's announcement. Write answers to these questions.

1. What do you like about the announcement?

2. What information is unclear?

3. What else do you want to know?

3 YOUR SECOND DRAFT

Use your partner's answers to revise your announcement.

① *BEFORE YOU WRITE*

Look at Paul's word web. Then read his letter to the editor. Number the topics in the order they appear in the letter.

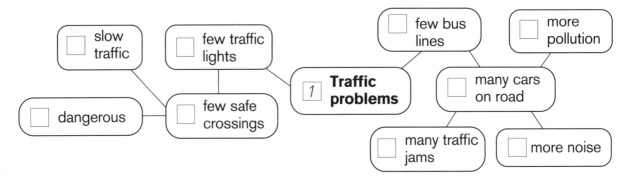

| slow traffic | few traffic lights | | few bus lines | | more pollution |

Dear Editor,
I'd like to complain about traffic problems in my neighborhood. First, there aren't enough traffic lights, so there are few safe crosswalks. This is dangerous for children and seniors. Also, it slows down the traffic. Second, there aren't enough bus lines, so there are too many cars on the road. As a result, there are more traffic jams. There is more noise and pollution, too.
I think the local council should find solutions to these problems.
Paul Hamilton
Spring Lane

② *YOUR FIRST DRAFT*

A Make a word web about a problem in your neighborhood. Use the word web in Exercise 1 as a model.

B Write a letter to the editor about the problem. Use the ideas from your word web and the letter in Exercise 1 as a model.

C *Pair work* Read your partner's word web and letter. Write answers to these questions.

1. What do you like about the letter?

2. Do the word web and the letter have the same information?

3. What else do you want to know?

③ *YOUR SECOND DRAFT*

Use your partner's answers to revise your letter.

1 BEFORE YOU WRITE

Read Susan's e-mail message. Complete the chart with information about Susan's apartment.

> Hello Sandy,
>
> Yes! We finally moved to our new apartment last week. We like the new place. It's new, and it's in a nice area of the city. More importantly, it's not as expensive as the old place. The rent is much lower.
> Of course, it's much smaller than the old place. It doesn't have as many windows, and there isn't enough closet space. But we're going to buy a new dresser, so that's OK.
> I just wish we had a bigger living room and more space for furniture, so we didn't have to sell our sofa.
> When are you going to come see our new place?
> Susan

Advantages	Disadvantages	Wishes
new		

2 YOUR FIRST DRAFT

A Make a chart about your apartment or house. Use the chart in Exercise 1 as a model.

B Imagine you have just moved to your apartment or house. Write an e-mail message to a friend about it. Use the information from your chart and the message in Exercise 1 as a model.

C *Pair work* Read your partner's message. Write answers to these questions.

1. What do you like about the message?

2. What information is unclear?

3. What else do you want to know?

3 YOUR SECOND DRAFT

Use your partner's answers to revise your message.

1 **BEFORE YOU WRITE**

A Match the healthy eating tips with the reasons.

1. Eat a good breakfast. _d_
2. Eat small portions several times a day. _____
3. Eat slowly. _____
4. Eat fruit and vegetables. _____
5. Drink a lot of water. _____

a. It cleans your body.
b. They have vitamins.
c. You never feel too hungry.
d. It gives you energy.
e. You eat less.

B Read the article and check your answers in part A.

Tips for healthy eating

First, eat a good breakfast. This gives you energy for the rest of the day. Second, eat small portions several times a day. That way, you are never too hungry and you don't overeat. Third, eat slowly. When you eat slowly, you eat less food and you enjoy it more. Next, eat plenty of fruit and vegetables. They are a good source of vitamins and complex carbohydrates. Finally, drink a lot of water. Water helps clean your system. Remember: You are what you eat!

2 **YOUR FIRST DRAFT**

A Make a list of tips for healthy eating or safe exercising. List a reason for each tip.

B Write a short article. Use your tips and the article in Exercise 1 as a model.

C *Pair work* Read your partner's article. Write answers to these questions.

1. What do you like about the article?
2. What information is unclear?
3. What else do you want to know?

3 **YOUR SECOND DRAFT**

Use your partner's answers to revise your article.

© Cambridge University Press Photocopiable

1 BEFORE YOU WRITE

Read the letter and check (✓) the correct boxes.

Dear Fred,
I'm very happy you're going to Los Palos with us for the weekend. We'll probably leave at around 6:00 P.M. on Friday. The trip will be about six hours, so I guess we'll stop for dinner on the way. We're going to rent a small cottage outside Los Palos.
It's very cold at this time of the year, so you'd better bring some warm clothes. And you should bring some good books, too. Los Palos is very quiet, so there's not very much to do!

See you on Friday! – Kate

	Plans	Possible plans	Advice
1. go to Los Palos	✓	☐	☐
2. leave at 6:00	☐	☐	☐
3. stop for dinner	☐	☐	☐
4. rent a cottage	☐	☐	☐
5. bring warm clothes	☐	☐	☐
6. bring good books	☐	☐	☐

2 YOUR FIRST DRAFT

A Complete the chart with plans for a vacation. Make notes about plans, possible plans, and advice.

Plans	Possible plans	Advice

B Imagine a friend is going with you on vacation. Write a letter describing your plans and giving advice. Use your notes and the letter in Exercise 1 as a model.

C *Pair work* Read your partner's letter. Write answers to these questions.

1. What do you like about the letter?

2. What information is unclear?

3. What else do you want to know?

3 YOUR SECOND DRAFT

Use your partner's answers to revise your letter.

Photocopiable

1 BEFORE YOU WRITE

A Mark and Peter share a house. Mark works during the day, and Peter works at night. Read each note and match it with the correct reply.

1. _____   2. _____   3. _____

| Mark,

Would you mind closing all the windows before you leave the house? You left the living room window open. When I got home, the neighbor's cats were on my bed!

Peter | Peter,

Would you please take the garbage out tomorrow before you go to work? The garbage collector only comes on Tuesdays and Fridays.

Mark | Mark,

Could you please put things back in the refrigerator after you use them? You didn't put the milk away, and today I had to throw it out.

Peter |

a.   b.   c.

| No problem. I'll make sure to take it out. | I'm sorry. I'll make sure I put everything away next time. | That's strange! I'm sure I closed it! |

B Read the notes again. Complete the chart.

	Request	**Reason**
1.	close all windows	neighbor's cats came in through window
2.		
3.		

2 YOUR FIRST DRAFT

A Make a chart with three requests and reasons for them. Use the chart in Exercise 1 as a model.

B Write three notes with your requests. Use the information from your chart and the notes in Exercise 1 as a model.

C *Pair work* Read your partner's notes. Write answers to these questions.

1. What do you like about the notes?

2. What information is unclear?

3. What else do you want to know?

4. Do you think the requests are reasonable?

3 YOUR SECOND DRAFT

A Use your partner's answers to revise your notes.

B *Pair work* Exchange notes. Write short replies to your partner's notes.

© Cambridge University Press   **Photocopiable**

BEFORE YOU WRITE

Louisa is going to house-sit for Lise while she's on vacation. Read Lise's message. How does she organize the information? Complete the sentences.

> Louisa,
> Thanks for offering to house-sit for me while I'm on vacation! Here are a few things to remember.
> 1. Make sure to feed the goldfish every morning. The food is in a small blue box on top of the refrigerator.
> 2. Remember to leave the keys with the neighbor on Wednesday. My brother's going to repair the refrigerator.
> 3. Don't forget to water the plants every evening.
> 4. Be sure to shop at the supermarket on Main Street. The smaller stores are very expensive.
> 5. The nearest bus stop is around the corner on Sixth Avenue. Number 24 goes downtown.
> 6. The neighborhood is safe, but be careful. Don't walk around alone late at night.
> Thanks again!
>
> Lise

Items ___1___ , _____ , and _____ are about the house.

Items _____ , _____ , and _____ are about the neighborhood.

2
YOUR FIRST DRAFT

A Imagine a friend is going to house-sit for you while you're on vacation. What does your friend need to know about the house or apartment and the neighborhood? Complete the chart.

About the house/apartment	About the neighborhood

B Write a message to your friend. Use your notes and the message in Exercise 1 as a model.

C *Pair work* Read your partner's message. Write answers to these questions.

1. What do you like about the message?

2. What information is unclear?

3. What else do you want to know?

3
YOUR SECOND DRAFT

Use your partner's answers to revise your message.

1 BEFORE YOU WRITE

Read the article and look at the events in **bold**. Underline the events that are also true in your country.

High school students in the U.S.

Before they graduate, many American **high school students find after-school jobs** and **get their driver's licenses**. They may also **take college entrance exams**, such as the SAT or ACT. About a month before graduation, **they attend the *prom*, a formal dance**. Boys rent tuxedos, and girls buy elegant evening gowns. Some look like Hollywood stars! When students graduate from high school, **there is a big ceremony**. Parents, grandparents, and other relatives attend. Many local communities **throw big parties** for the graduates. After graduation, **some graduates go to a four-year university**. **Others go to trade schools** and become electricians or hair stylists. **Others enter the military**. **Still others get jobs that don't require additional education**.

---

2 YOUR FIRST DRAFT

A Complete the chart with information about high school students in your country.

Before graduation	Graduation	After graduation

B Write an article about high school students in your country. Write one paragraph about life before graduation, one about graduation, and one about life after graduation. Use your notes and the article in Exercise 1 as a model.

C *Pair work* Read your partner's article. Write answers to these questions.

1. What do you like about the article?

2. What information is unclear?

3. What else do you want to know?

3 YOUR SECOND DRAFT

Use your partner's answers to revise your article.

© Cambridge University Press   Photocopiable

1 BEFORE YOU WRITE

A Read the letter and reply. Do you agree with Clara's advice?

Dear Clara,	Dear Linda,
I work in a store. My salary is low and the job is boring, but it's secure. Today I got an offer for a more exciting job with a better salary. But I'm afraid to change jobs. What should I do? – Linda	There are three things you can do. You can stay in your job, you can accept the offer, or you can ask for time to think about it. If you stay in your job, you won't take any risks. If you accept the new job, you will feel less secure. If you ask for more time, someone else may get the job. So here's my advice. If you listen to your heart, you'll know what to do! Good luck! – Clara

B Read Clara's reply again. Complete the chart.

	Possible actions	Consequences
1.	Stay in your job	You won't take any risks.
2.		
3.		

2 YOUR FIRST DRAFT

A Imagine you are Clara. Choose a letter below and make a chart with possible actions and consequences. Use the chart in Exercise 1 as a model.

Dear Clara, I think my girlfriend doesn't love me anymore. What should I do? – Paul	Dear Clara, I live with my parents and I hate it! What should I do? – Linda	Dear Clara, I hate my school! What should I do? – Rick

B Write a reply to the letter you chose. Use the information from your chart and the reply in Exercise 1 as a model.

C *Pair work* Read your partner's reply. Write answers to these questions.

1. What do you like about the reply?

2. What information is unclear?

3. What else do you want to know?

3 YOUR SECOND DRAFT

Use your partner's answers to revise your reply.

① BEFORE YOU WRITE

Read the ads and answer the questions.

a.

TRUCK DRIVERS
We
• are a successful transport company.
• have been in the business for over 20 years.
• offer excellent income potential.
You
• are honest and reliable.
• have a commercial driver's license.
• enjoy driving long distances.
Send résumé to *International Transport, P.O. Box 555, Seattle, Washington.*

b.

Looking for truck drivers
A transport company is looking for truck drivers. Please don't contact us if you are not honest and hardworking. You also must have a commercial driver's license. You will have to drive over a thousand kilometers a day. Send résumé to *International Transport, P.O. Box 555, Seattle, Washington.*

1. Which ad is easier to read? _____

2. Which ad suggests the salary may be good? _____

3. Which ad suggests the job may be hard? _____

4. Which ad do you prefer? _____

② YOUR FIRST DRAFT

A Imagine you own a company. You want to hire someone for a position with your company. Make notes about your company and the position.

B Write an ad. Use the ad you preferred in Exercise 1 as a model.

C *Pair work* Read your partner's ad. Write answers to these questions.

1. What do you like about the ad?

2. What information is unclear?

3. What else do you want to know?

③ YOUR SECOND DRAFT

Use your partner's answers to revise your ad.

© Cambridge University Press   **Photocopiable**

1 ① BEFORE YOU WRITE

A Read the brochure. Write the correct heading from the box above each paragraph.

Attractions	Location	History

THE EMPIRE STATE BUILDING

_____

1 The Empire State Building was built during the Depression between 1920 and 1931. The building was officially opened by President Herbert Hoover on May 31, 1931. In 1945, the 79th floor was damaged when an Army Corps B 25 crashed into it. Fourteen people were killed, but the structure wasn't damaged.

_____

2 Over 3.5 million people visit the Empire State Building every year. The main tourist attraction is the Observatory on the 86th floor. It offers a fantastic view of Manhattan. The building is also visited for its restaurants and art exhibitions.

_____

3 The Empire State Building is located at 350 5th Avenue. You can get there by subway (lines 1, 2, 3, and 9) or by bus (M4, M10, M34, and Q32).

B Read the brochure again and underline all the passive verbs.

2 ② YOUR FIRST DRAFT

A Choose a landmark in your country. Complete the chart with information about the landmark.

Attractions	Location	History

B Write a brochure for the landmark you chose. Write one paragraph about its attractions, one about its location, and one about its history. Use your notes and the brochure in Exercise 1 as a model.

C *Pair work* Read your partner's brochure. Write answers to these questions.

1. What do you like about the brochure?

2. What information is unclear?

3. What else do you want to know?

3 ③ YOUR SECOND DRAFT

Use your partner's answers to revise your brochure.

1 ❶ *BEFORE YOU WRITE*

Read the cover letter for a job application. Number the topics in the order they appear.

Dear Sir or Madam,

Please consider my résumé for the bilingual camp counselor position advertised on your Web page. As my résumé shows, I am very qualified for this position. My first language is Spanish, and I speak English fluently. I have been working with children since elementary school, when I began babysitting. In addition, three years ago I was senior counselor at a summer camp. I have just completed a Bachelor of Arts degree in child psychology, and I am now looking for a position where I can apply my experience and education.

I am very interested in this position. If you would like me to come in for an interview, you can reach me at 555-1785. I look forward to hearing from you.

Yours sincerely,
Raul Alarcón

☐ request for an interview

☐ job he's applying for

☐ relevant experience

2 ❷ *YOUR FIRST DRAFT*

A Imagine you are applying for your ideal job. Make notes about your relevant experience.

B Write a cover letter. Use your notes and the letter in Exercise 1 as a model.

C *Pair work* Read your partner's letter. Write answers to these questions.

1. What do you like about the letter?

2. What information is unclear?

3. What else do you want to know?

3 ❸ *YOUR SECOND DRAFT*

Use your partner's answers to revise your letter.

① BEFORE YOU WRITE

Read the book review. How is it organized? Check (✓) the correct diagram.

Life in Hooverville
by Richard Reynolds

Michael Robinson has been managing the town's diner for 20 years. He does not like his job, and he wants to move to the big city. However, he stays in the town because of the people there. There's Trish, his daughter, who is having problems in high school. There's Jane, his ex-wife. And there's Felicia Whittaker, the woman who owns everything in town.

This is probably Reynolds' best novel. In it, he draws a fascinating picture of life in a typical American small town. The story moves a little slowly, but the character development is excellent. I think it is one of the greatest novels of the 21st century.

☐ 1.
- Title
- Author
- Plot
- Reviewer's opinions

☐ 2.
- Title
- Author
- Reviewer's opinions
- Plot

② YOUR FIRST DRAFT

A Complete the chart with information about a book you read.

Title: _____ Author: _____

Main events: _____

Things you liked: _____

Things you didn't like: _____

B Write a review of the book you chose. Use the information from your chart and the review in Exercise 1 as a model.

C *Pair work* Read your partner's review. Write answers to these questions.

1. What do you like about the review?

2. What information is unclear?

3. What else do you want to know?

③ YOUR SECOND DRAFT

Use your partner's answers to revise your review.

1 *BEFORE YOU WRITE*

Read the traffic rules and answer the questions.

City Traffic Rules

a. You have to obey the street signs.

b. You aren't allowed to drive through a red light.

c. You can park in the parking garages.

d. You can't drive more than 30 miles an hour.

e. You're allowed to turn right on red.

f. You have to carry your driver's license.

_____ 1. Which rules express permission?

_____ 2. Which rules express obligation?

_____ 3. Which rules express prohibition?

2 *YOUR FIRST DRAFT*

A Write a list of six traffic rules for your city or town. Use the rules in Exercise 1 as a model.

B *Pair work* Read your partner's list. Write answers to these questions.

1. What do you like about the list?

2. What information is unclear?

3. What else do you want to know?

3 *YOUR SECOND DRAFT*

Use your partner's answers to revise your list.

BEFORE YOU WRITE

Read the e-mail messages. Check (✓) the correct boxes.

From: Bob Jones	From: Andrea Dalton
To: Andrea Dalton	To: Bob Jones
Subject: Help!	Subject: RE: Help!
Hi Andrea, I made a terrible mistake. I asked my boss for a raise. I said if she couldn't pay me more, I would look for another job. She said, "Maybe you should start looking for another job now." But I don't want another job! I just need more money for rent. What should I do? – Bob	Hi Bob, You shouldn't have said that. I would have told my boss about the problem with the rent. Then I would have asked for help. Why don't you talk to her again and explain why you need a raise? More important, tell her you don't want another job. Good luck! – Andrea

Who . . . ?	Bob	Andrea
1. describes a problem	☐	☐
2. criticizes someone	☐	☐
3. gives advice	☐	☐

YOUR FIRST DRAFT

A Imagine a friend sent you this e-mail message. Answer the questions.

I worked very hard in a course, but my teacher gave me a low grade. When I asked for a higher grade, my teacher gave me a failing grade! What should I do?

1. Did your friend do the right thing?

_____

2. What would you have done differently?

_____

3. What should your friend do now?

_____

B Write an e-mail message to your friend. Use your notes and the message in Exercise 1 as a model.

C *Pair work* Read your partner's message. Write answers to these questions.

1. What do you like about the message?

2. What information is unclear?

3. What else do you want to know?

YOUR SECOND DRAFT

Use your partner's answers to revise your message.

BEFORE YOU WRITE

Read the notes. Match each note with a purpose from the box.

to ask for a favor	to complain	to invite
to ask for information	to give a warning	to make an offer

Bob, Last night you were playing your violin until 3:00 A.M. I couldn't sleep at all. Why don't you stop? Helen	Mary Ann, Yesterday you told me about a pet shop near the office. Where is it exactly? I need to buy a new toothbrush for my dog. Fred

1. _____to complain_____   2. _____

Pete, You said you wanted a laptop computer. I've just bought a new laptop, and I don't need the old one anymore. Would you like to use it? Linda	Joe, This morning you said you were too sick to come to work. But then I saw you walking around the mall! Please see me in my office. This can't happen again! Ms. Grant

3. _____   4. _____

Jim, I'm having a dinner party tomorrow night. My friends from school will be there. Would you like to join us? Melissa	Sarah, I need to return this book to the library, but I forgot I had a dentist appointment. Could you return it for me? Thanks! Hiro

5. _____   6. _____

YOUR FIRST DRAFT

A Write four notes to people you know. Use a different purpose for each note.

B *Pair work* Read your partner's notes. Write answers to these questions.

1. What do you like about the notes?

2. What information is unclear?

3. What else do you want to know?

YOUR SECOND DRAFT

A Use your partner's answers to revise your notes.

B *Pair work* Exchange notes. Write short replies to your partner's notes.

            Photocopiable

1 PERSONAL AD

Aim: *Give Ss practice exchanging personal information.*
Preparation: *Make one copy of Project 1 for every S.*
Materials: *Colored pencils or pens*

Plan
- Give each S a handout. As a class, brainstorm topics and write them on the board. If necessary, refer Ss to the Snapshot on page 2 of the Student's Book.
- Explain the task. Ss write a question for each topic.

Prepare
- Ss work in pairs. Explain the task. Ss interview each other and write a personal ad for their partner. Encourage Ss to use photos or drawings.

Present
- Have Ss introduce their partner by showing their ads to the class. Encourage other Ss to ask questions.
- Ask Ss to create a class Web site with links to each student's personal ad.

2 THIS TRAFFIC IS FRUSTRATING!

Aim: *Give Ss practice using talking about transportation using adverbs of quantity.*
Preparation: *Make one copy of Project 2 for every 2 Ss.*
Materials: *None*

Plan
- Give each pair a handout and explain the task. Ss write three transportation problems. Then discuss the problems as a class.
- Brainstorm alternative forms of transportation (e.g., *electric cars, trolleys, diesel buses, hydrogen cars, hybrid cars, monorails, commuter trains*). If necessary, refer Ss to the Reading on page 13 of the Student's Book.

Prepare
- Each pair joins another pair. Explain the task. Ss choose and research one type of transportation.
- ***Option:*** Assign each group a form of transportation.
- Ss write a letter explaining how the form of transportation is the best choice for their city or town. Refer Ss to the Writing on page 10 of the Student's Book. Encourage them to use adverbs of quantity to describe transportation problems.

Present
- Have Ss read their letters to the class. Encourage other Ss to ask questions.
- Take a class vote on the best solution for the city's problems.

3 ADDING UP THE COSTS

Aim: *Give Ss practice talking about living expenses.*
Preparation: *Make one copy of Project 3 for every S.*
Materials: *Poster paper; colored pencils or pens*

Plan
- Write this sentence on the board:
Teenagers should pay their parents rent to live at home.
- Ask the class: "Do you agree with this statement?" Elicit answers and reasons.
- Give each S a handout and explain the task. Ss complete the chart with their monthly expenses. Elicit suggestions (e.g., *food, rent, transportation, entertainment, clothing*). Remind Ss to consider everything they spend money on.

Prepare
A
- Explain the task. Ss find the actual cost of each item. Explain that Ss may have to ask other members of their household for information about actual costs.
- Have Ss present their findings in two separate charts (e.g., *bar, pie, line graph*).

B
- Divide the class into groups. Ss share their charts and discuss the original statement.

Present
- Divide the class into two teams. Team A agrees with the statement and Team B disagrees. Have a class debate.

4 WHAT DO THEY EAT THERE?

Aim: *Give Ss practice describing recipes using sequence adverbs.*
Preparation: *Make one copy of Project 4 for every S.*
Materials: *None*

Plan
- Give each S a handout. Discuss the questions as a class. Elicit answers.
- Ss write a list of ingredients for a dish.

Prepare
- Divide the class into small groups. Explain the task. Ss decide on a country. Then they research its cuisine and choose a traditional dish.
- Have Ss write a list of ingredients and recipe for the dish. Encourage them to use photos or draw pictures of the dish.

Present
- Have Ss share their recipes with the class and demonstrate how to make the dish.
- ***Option:*** Have Ss make the dish at home and bring it to class.
- ***Option:*** Collect the recipes to make a class cookbook.

5 WHEN IN ROME . . .

Aim: *Give Ss practice giving travel advice using modals for necessity and suggestion.*
Preparation: *Make one copy of Project 5 for every group.*
Materials: *None*

Plan
- Divide the class into small groups. Give each group a handout. Ss discuss the questions.
- Elicit examples of how dos and don'ts vary from country to country.

Prepare
- Explain the task. Ss choose a country and research the dos and don'ts of travel there.
- *Option:* Assign each group a country.
- Ss write a list of guidelines for travelers. Encourage Ss to include photos or drawings to explain the rules.

Present
- Have groups share their guidelines with the class. Encourage Ss to use modals for necessity and suggestion (e.g., *You shouldn't eat on the street.*).
- *Option:* Collect the lists to make a class travel guide.

6 PET PEEVES

Aim: *Give Ss practice making complaints.*
Preparation: *Make one copy of Project 6 for every S.*
Materials: *None*

Plan
- Give each S a handout. Ask: "What is a pet peeve?" Elicit or explain the meaning. Then elicit pet peeves from the class.
- As a class, divide the complaints into categories (e.g., *friends, family, school, teachers, neighbors, traffic, cell phones, computers*) and write them on the board.

Prepare
- Divide the class into small groups. Explain the task. Ss choose a category of complaints.
- Each group asks 100 people the same question and records how many respondents give the same answer.

Present
- Play a game. Groups read their questions. Other Ss try to guess the top five answers to the question.

 ## 7 I HATE CLEANING!

Aim: *Give Ss practice using infinitives and gerunds.*
Preparation: *Make one copy of Project 7 for every S.*
Materials: *Poster paper; colored pencils or pens*

Plan
- Give each S a handout. As a class, brainstorm chores Ss hate to do. Elicit reasons.
- Have Ss write their least favorite chores and reasons.

Prepare
- Divide the class into small groups. Explain the task. Ss choose one chore they dislike.
- Ask Ss to design an invention to perform the activity.
- Have Ss make an ad for the invention. Encourage them to draw pictures and to describe what the device can do.

Present
- Have groups share their inventions with the class. Encourage them to describe how the invention works and what it could be used for.

8 UNUSUAL CELEBRATIONS

Aim: *Give Ss practice describing holidays.*
Preparation: *Make one copy of Project 8 for every S.*
Materials: *Poster paper; colored pencils or pens*

Plan
- Give each S a handout and go over the questions. Explain the task. Ss choose a celebration and answer the questions.
- Elicit answers from the class.

Prepare
A
- Divide the class into small groups. Have Ss choose a country and research an unusual celebration there. Encourage Ss to use books, magazines, or the Internet to find the information.

B
- Have Ss prepare a presentation about this celebration. Remind them to use pictures, costumes, food, or music to explain the tradition.

Present
- Have groups present the celebration to the class. Encourage other Ss to ask questions.

       Photocopiable

9 HISTORICAL EVENTS

Aim: *Give Ss practice comparing time periods.*
Preparation: *Make one copy of Project 9 for every two Ss.*
Materials: *Poster paper; colored pencils or pens*

Plan
- Ss work in pairs. Give each pair a handout. Ss answer the questions. Encourage them to think about events that may have future consequences (e.g., *James Watt's improvements on the steam engine led to the Industrial Revolution.*).
- Elicit events and reasons from the class.

Prepare
A
- Each pair joins another pair. Explain the task. Groups choose and research five events. Remind them to find photos or draw pictures to represent each event.
- Have Ss create a time line including the events and when they occurred.

B
- Ask Ss to predict five future events and add them to the time line.

Present
- Have groups share their time lines with the class. Remind them to explain why the past events were significant and how they predicted the future.

10 WHAT'S A GOOD JOB FOR ME?

Aim: *Give Ss practice talking about job preferences.*
Preparation: *Make one copy of Project 10 for every S.*
Materials: *None*

Plan
- Give each S a handout. If necessary, elicit or explain what a career counselor does.
- As a class, brainstorm the kinds of things a career counselor might ask about (e.g., *interests, skills, experiences, preferences*).

Prepare
A
- Divide the class into small groups. Explain the task. Ss write survey questions to determine someone's ideal career. Explain that Ss should write at least 15 open-ended or multiple-choice questions.

B
- Have groups exchange surveys, answer the questions, and return them to the original group.
- Groups read the answers and determine a suitable career for each S.

Present
- Have groups explain their decisions to the class.

11 IN HONOR OF . . .

Aim: *Give Ss practice talking about landmarks using the passive.*
Preparation: *Make one copy of Project 11 for every S.*
Materials: *Poster paper; colored pencils or pens*

Plan
- Give Ss a handout and focus their attention on the pictures. Ask: "What is a monument? Why are monuments built?"
- As a class, discuss the questions. Elicit answers. Encourage Ss to use the passive (e.g., *It was built for... It was designed by...*).

Prepare
- Divide the class into small groups. Explain the task. Ss design a monument for their city or town. Encourage Ss to create something symbolic or relevant to where they live.
- *Option:* Have Ss build a model of the monument.

Present
- Have groups share their monuments with the class. Remind them to explain the symbolism and relevance of the design.
- *Option:* Take a class vote on the best monument for the city or town.

12 WHAT HAPPENED NEXT?

Aim: *Give Ss practice telling stories*
Preparation: *Make one copy of Project 12 for every group.*
Materials: *None*

Plan
- Divide the class into small groups. Give each group a handout and focus their attention on the pictures. Ask: "What do you see?" Elicit descriptions.
- Ss write three things about each photo.

Prepare
A
- Explain the task. Ss look for two pictures of people, places, or things. Explain that the pictures should not have anything to do with each other.

B
- Ask groups to exchange pictures. Then Ss write a story connecting the two pictures. Encourage Ss to be creative and imagine other characters or events that are not in the pictures.
- If necessary, use the photos on the handout to model the beginning of a story.

Present
- Have groups tell their stories to the class. Then Ss vote on the most creative and the funniest story.

THE ACTING WAS FANTASTIC!

Aim: *Give Ss practice talking about movies.*
Preparation: *Make one copy of Project 13 for every group.*
Materials: *None*

Plan

- Divide the class into small groups. Give each group a handout. Ss choose a movie they want to watch. Explain that it can be a movie that's already out on video/DVD or a new movie that's still playing in theaters.

Prepare

- Explain the task. Ss decide on a scene to perform for the class. Explain that they can find the original script or create a script from memory. Encourage Ss to use costumes, props, and music.
- Have Ss practice the scene before the performance.

Present

- Have groups perform their scenes for the class. Encourage other groups to use the questions to rate the performance and give feedback.

⑭ PROVERB PUZZLE

Aim: *Give Ss practice explaining meaning using modals and adverbs.*
Preparation: *Make one copy of Project 14 for every S.*
Materials: *Poster paper; colored pencils or pens*

Plan

- Give each S a handout and focus their attention on the picture. Discuss the question as a class.
- Have Ss write three proverbs and their meanings. Encourage them to think of proverbs from their own country. If necessary, tell Ss to ask friends or relatives for ideas.

Prepare

- Divide the class into small groups. Explain the task. Ss compare their proverbs. Then groups choose one proverb to illustrate for the class.
- Have Ss create a poster that illustrates the proverb. Remind them to represent the proverb using pictures, not words.

Present

- Put the posters on the classroom walls. Ask the class to look at each illustration and guess the meaning.
- Elicit guesses from the class. Encourage Ss to use modals and adverbs to guess meaning (e.g., *It might mean..., It could mean..., Maybe it means...*).

⑮ WOULD YOU DO IT?

Aim: *Give Ss practice describing predicaments.*
Preparation: *Make one copy of Project 15 for every S.*
Materials: *Six index cards (or paper cut into cards) for every S*

Plan

- Give each S a handout. As a class, brainstorm examples of predicaments (e.g., *You find a wallet with $500 in it.*).

Prepare

- Divide the class into small groups. Explain the task. Groups write three situations for each S in the group. Remind them to write each situation and its yes/no question on a separate card.
- Have Ss make three answer cards by each writing *Yes*, *No*, or *Depends* on each card.
- Remind Ss that they should each have six cards.

Present

- Collect the cards and divide them into two piles: situations and answers.
- Go over the rules on the handout as a class. Then play the game.

COULD YOU . . . ?

Aim: *Give Ss practice making reported requests and statements.*
Preparation: *Make one copy of Project 16 for every S.*
Materials: *None*

Plan

- Give each S a handout and go over the questions. Elicit situations.
- Discuss the questions as a class.

Prepare

- Divide the class into small groups. Explain the task. Each S chooses a request.
- Outside of class, Ss call five different people, make the request, and write the responses.
- Ss compare their experiences with the group. Encourage them to use reported speech to tell what each person said.

Present

- Have Ss share their findings with the class. Encourage other Ss to ask questions.
- If a request was refused, ask the class: "Do you believe the excuse?"

PERSONAL AD

About Me

Gender:	male
Location:	New York, NY
Age:	25
Marital status:	single – never married
Body type:	athletic
Height:	6'0"
Eyes:	brown
Hair:	dark brown
Personality:	clever; shy
Living situation:	with roommate
Education:	college graduate
Occupation:	artist / musician / writer
Astrology:	capricorn
Languages:	English
Interests:	art, dining, photography, watching sports, theater, travel, cooking, computers/Internet, crafts, playing sports, health/fitness

In my own words:
I do many things in the city to stay busy, so if you're curious then just ask! All you get is me, so just be you… and it'll be great. Talk to you soon!

Plan

What kind of information do people usually include in a personal ad?
Write six topics.

1. _____   4. _____

2. _____   5. _____

3. _____   6. _____

For each topic, write one question to ask someone for personal information.

1. _____

2. _____

3. _____

4. _____

5. _____

6. _____

Prepare

Pair work Use the questions to interview your partner. Remember to take notes.
Then use the information to design an online personal ad for your partner.

Present

Class activity Introduce your partner to the class. Show your personal ad and
answer questions. Then create a class Web site with links to each student's ad.

Plan

Pair work Write three transportation problems in your city or town.

1. _____
2. _____
3. _____

Write three alternative forms of transportation.

1. _____
2. _____
3. _____

Prepare

Group work Choose an alternative form of transportation you are interested in learning more about. Then write a letter to the city explaining how you think this form of transportation will help improve the city's problems.

Present

Class activity Share your letter with the class. Which form of transportation do you think is the best solution for the city's transportation problems? Take a class vote.

     Photocopiable

ADDING UP THE COSTS

Plan

Make a list of all the things you spend money on each month. Then estimate the monthly cost of each item.

Expense	Cost	Expense	Cost

Prepare

A Find out how much you spend every month. Then draw two charts. Display your original prediction in one chart and your actual expenses in the other.

B *Group work* Share your charts with the group. Based on your findings, do you agree or disagree that teenagers should pay rent?

Present

Class activity Have a debate. Team A argues that teenagers living at home should pay rent. Team B disagrees. Use the information in your charts to support your argument. Try to convince the other team that you are right!

WHAT DO THEY EAT THERE?

Plan

What is a traditional dish from your country? Do you know how to prepare it?
Write the name of the dish. Then make a list of the ingredients you need to
make it.

Dish: _____

Ingredients: _____   _____

_____   _____

_____   _____

Prepare

Group work Choose a country you want to learn more about. Then research a
traditional dish from that country. Make a list of ingredients and write a recipe
for the dish.

Present

Class activity Share your recipe with the class. Then demonstrate how to prepare
the dish. Remember to bring the ingredients and materials necessary to make it!

Plan

Group work Discuss these questions.

How do people greet each other in your country?

What is something people do in your country, but *shouldn't* do in other countries?

What is something people do in other countries, but *shouldn't* do in your country?

Prepare

Group work Choose a country you are interested in learning more about. Research things you *should* and *shouldn't* do there. For example, how should you dress, greet people, and behave in public? Make a list of guidelines for travel in that country.

Present

Class activity Imagine your class will travel to this country. Share your guidelines with the class. Be sure to warn them about what they should and shouldn't do!

 **PET PEEVES**

Plan

Class activity What is your pet peeve? Compare your ideas with the class.

What kinds of pet peeves does the class have? Divide the complaints into categories.

_____   _____

_____   _____

_____   _____

Prepare

Group work Choose a category and complete the survey question below. As a group, ask 100 people the question. Make sure to write their answers. Then order the answers from most common to least common.

Start with this question:

What is your biggest complaint / pet peeve about . . . ?

Present

Class activity Play a game. Share your survey question with the class. Other groups try to guess the five most common answers.

© Cambridge University Press   **Photocopiable**

I HATE CLEANING!

Plan

What are some chores that you hate to do? Why do you dislike them?

	Chore	Reason
1.		
2.		
3.		

Prepare

Group work Choose a chore that you dislike and design an invention to do it for you. Then make an advertisement. Be sure to draw a picture of your invention and list its features.

Present

Class activity Share your invention with the class. Explain how it works and what it can be used for.

UNUSUAL CELEBRATIONS

Punxsutawney Phil on Groundhog Day

Plan

Think of an unusual celebration in your country. Answer these questions.

Who celebrates it? _____

Where is it celebrated? _____

Why is it celebrated? _____

Prepare

A *Group work* Choose a country you want to learn more about. Then research an interesting celebration in that country. Use these questions and your own questions.

Why is it celebrated?

How is it celebrated?

What do people wear?

What do people eat?

Is there any music or a special ceremony?

B *Group work* Prepare a presentation about the celebration. Use pictures, costumes, food, or music to present the information you learned. Be creative!

Present

Class activity Explain the celebration to the class. Share what you learned and be prepared to answer questions.

© Cambridge University Press   Photocopiable

1775: James Watt invents the first
reliable steam engine.

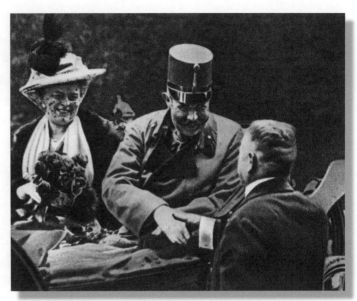

June 28, 1914: Assassination of Archduke
Franz Ferdinand

Plan

Pair work Think of three important historical events. Why do you think they
are important?

	Event	Reason
1.		
2.		
3.		

Prepare

A *Group work* Choose five important historical events and research information
about them. Then make a time line showing when the events occurred. Use pictures
to represent each event.

B *Group work* Predict five events that you think will happen in the future. Add
them to your time line.

Present

Class activity Share your time line with the class. Explain the significance of each
event and how you predicted future events.

10 WHAT'S A GOOD JOB FOR ME?

Plan

Have you even spoken with a career counselor? What things do you think this person asks someone looking for the right career? Write three things.

1. _____

2. _____

3. _____

Prepare

A *Group work* Imagine you are career counselors. Create a survey to help someone decide on a suitable career. Write at least 15 questions.

Start with these questions:

What do you like to do more than anything?
I'd prefer to work a) at home. b) in an office. c) outdoors.

B *Group work* Ask another group to complete your quiz. Then collect the answers and decide on the best career for each person.

Present

Class activity Share your decisions with the class. Explain why you think the career you chose for each student is suitable. Have fun with the recommendations!

The Washington Monument

The Taj Mahal

The Sphinx

Plan

Choose three examples of famous monuments. Why was each monument built?

	Monument	Reason
1.		
2.		
3.		

Prepare

Group work Imagine you are city planners. Design a monument for the city or town where you live. Use these questions and your own ideas.

Who or what will the monument honor?

Where will you build it?

What will it look like?

How big will it be?

What will it be made of?

Present

Class activity Share your monument with the class. Explain why you chose the design.

Picture 1

Picture 2

Plan

Group work Look at the pictures. Then write three things you see in each photo.

	Picture 1	Picture 2
1.		
2.		
3.		

Prepare

A *Group work* Use magazine, newspapers, or your own photos to find two interesting pictures of people, places, or things. Bring them to class.

B *Group work* Exchange pictures with another group. Then write a story to connect the two pictures. Be creative! You can add characters or events that are not in the pictures to make the story more interesting.

Present

Class activity Share your pictures and story with the class. Which story is the most creative? Which is the funniest? Take a class vote.

THE ACTING WAS FANTASTIC!

Plan

Group work Choose a movie that you all want to see. Rent the movie or find out when and where it's playing. Then watch the movie together.

Movie: _____

Prepare

Group work Discuss your favorite scenes from the movie. Then choose one scene to act out for the class. Assign roles and rehearse the scene. Use costumes, props, and music to make your performance more interesting.

Present

Class activity Perform your scene for the class. Then use these questions to rate the other performances.

How was the acting?

Were the costumes appropriate?

Was music used? Did it make the scene more effective?

What aspects of the performance did you like best?

What aspects of the performance could be improved?

14 *PROVERB PUZZLE*

Plan

Look at the picture. What do you think the proverb *There's no use crying over spilled milk* means?

Write three proverbs you know.

1. _____

2. _____

3. _____

Write the meaning of each proverb.

1. _____

2. _____

3. _____

Prepare

Group work Choose one proverb to share with the class. Then make a poster to explain the proverb. Draw pictures, but don't write the proverb!

Present

Class activity Look at the posters. Can you guess the meaning of each picture? Can you guess the proverb?

© Cambridge University Press   **Photocopiable**

WOULD YOU DO IT?

Plan

Think of a predicament involving a difficult decision. Then share your situation with the class.

Prepare

Group work For each student in the group, write three situations followed by a *yes/no* question. Write each on a separate card.

Start with a situation and question like this:

You find a wallet with $500 in it. The street is empty, so no one sees you pick it up. You really need the money to pay your rent. Would you keep the money?

Then make three answer cards for each student in the group. Write YES, NO, or DEPENDS on each card.

Present

Class activity Play the game.

1. Place the cards face-down in two piles: situations and answers.

2. Take three situation cards and one answer card. Look at your cards, but don't show them to anyone.

3. Take turns. Read one of your situation cards to any other player.

4. If that player's answer matches **your** answer card, you discard that situation card. Do not take another card.

5. If the player's answer does *not* match your answer card, you discard that situation card and take another one from the pile.

6. Always discard your answer card after your turn and take a new one.

7. Put used answer and situation cards face-up in a pile. Shuffle and reuse them if you run out.

8. Players who answer DEPENDS must always explain their answer.

9. The first player to get rid of all three situation cards wins.

Plan

Think of a situation when you were asked to do something you didn't want to do. What was the request? What did you say?

Prepare

Group work Choose a request. Then call five different people and make the request. Write the responses and excuses to show the group. Use these requests or your own ideas.

Can you help me move?   Can you help me paint this weekend?

Could you help me study?   Could you pick me up at the airport?

Could you lend me $100?   Can I borrow your new leather jacket?

Could you type my report?   Can you make me a copy of a CD/DVD?

Can you take a test for me?   Could you water my plants while I'm away?

Could you baby-sit for me?   Could you tell my boss/teacher that I'm sick?

Present

Class activity Share your findings with the class. Use reported speech to explain your request and the responses. How many people refused your request? What were their excuses?

ANSWER KEY LISTENING (WITH AUDIO SCRIPTS)

Unit 1

Audio Script

Interview about the past [Track 1]

B Listen to the interviews. Check true or false.

Huang

DANIEL: When did you move to Canada, Huang?

Huang: When I was three. My parents came from Vietnam. My father used to be a teacher, and my mother used to work in a bank.

DANIEL: Do you remember much about Vietnam?

HUANG: No, not really. I was too young to remember much. But I do remember certain things about it. We used to have a lovely, old house near a river. There was a beautiful flowering tree in our garden. And I can remember the scent of the soap my grandmother used to use.

DANIEL: That's nice. Did your grandmother use to live with you?

HUANG: Yes, she did. She still lives there. I'd love to go back and visit her sometime.

DANIEL: And were you always good at music?

HUANG: Well, yeah.

DANIEL: When did you learn the piano?

HUANG: I started when I was six. We had a terrible, old piano that I tried to play.

DANIEL: Did your parents play?

HUANG: No, but my dad was a really good singer. Then my parents bought a new piano and decided I should have lessons. I had a really great teacher. She was from Italy. I used to go to her house for lessons.

DANIEL: And when did you give your first concert?

HUANG: When I was 11.

DANIEL: Wow.

Pedro

DANIEL: Where did you grow up, Pedro?

PEDRO: I grew up near Chicago.

DANIEL: And what did you major in at college?

PEDRO: Physical education. I really wanted to be a gym teacher at a school. I love sports, and I used to play them a lot.

DANIEL: So what made you change your mind?

PEDRO: After I graduated, I tried to get a job as a gym teacher in my town, but I couldn't. I didn't want to move away because my father was sick. So I had to find something else to do.

DANIEL: So how did you get into the restaurant business?

PEDRO: Well, I was always kind of interested in cooking. My mom taught me to cook, and I often used to make meals for the family when I was a kid. Anyway, my dad's friend had a small restaurant, and he asked me if I'd like to help out. My first job was helping in the kitchen, and that's where I really learned to cook. I used to watch the chefs at work so that I could pick up their techniques. Then a year later, the owner asked me to be one of the chefs!

DANIEL: And how long ago was that?

PEDRO: That was five years ago. Then a couple of years ago, I decided to open up my own restaurant. It's done really well. We have three chefs, and we're usually very busy – especially on the weekends.

DANIEL: Good for you!

C Listen again. Answer the questions.

Answer Key

A
Answers will vary.

B

Huang
1. F   2. T   3. T   4. F   5. T

Pedro
1. F   2. T   3. F   4. F   5. F

C

Huang
1. Her mother used to work in a bank.
2. She used to take piano lessons at her teacher's house.
3. She gave her first concert when she was 11.

Pedro
1. He used to play sports.
2. His mother taught him.
3. He used to watch the chefs.

D
Answers will vary.

Unit 2

Audio Script

City problems [Track 2]

B Listen to the conversations about problems in a city. Number the pictures from 1 to 3.

1.

WOMAN 1: That's why the air quality is so bad around here. It's not good for people's health. There are too many factories in the area. I think they should move them away from the city.

WOMAN 2: Yes! And it's getting worse and worse. They're all pumping dangerous chemicals into the air! There are no controls on industries. But how can we stop them?

WOMAN 1: They should start fining the companies that are responsible. That's what they should do. It's the only way they'll get them to change.

2.

MAN: There are too many trucks and vans on the roads. They're the cause of the problem. I think they should keep trucks out of the city during rush hour. That's why we have this terrible problem.

WOMAN: I agree. But also there are too many cars on the roads, and most of them have only one person in them. They should only allow you to drive into the city if you have a full car. It's ridiculous to have all these cars driving around with only one person in them.

3.

MAN: It's very difficult to cross the streets because there aren't enough of them. People risk their lives trying to cross the street whenever there's a break in the traffic. It's crazy! No wonder there are so many accidents.

WOMAN: Yeah, they should put in a lot more. There aren't enough on the major streets, especially downtown.

MAN: And if drivers don't stop when people are trying to cross, they should get a huge fine. Lots of drivers just go straight through them, even when people are trying to cross.

WOMAN: You're telling me! I almost got hit today!

MAN: Oh, no!

C Listen again. Check the two solutions suggested for each problem.

Answer Key
A
Answers will vary.
B
3, 1, 2
C
1. a, c   2. a, b   3. a, c

Unit 3

Audio Script
How did you like the apartment? [Track 3]

B Listen to Mark and Louise discuss the apartments they visited. Check true or false.

1.
MARK: So, how did you like the apartment?
LOUISE: Well, I liked some things. The kitchen has lots of room – I hate small kitchens! And this is an interesting neighborhood. It's very lively, with all the students around.
MARK: Yeah, it is. I'm worried about the bedroom, though. I don't think we could manage with just one bedroom. Especially since your relatives come to stay all the time.
LOUISE: True. I guess we'd need to spend money on furniture, too, since it only has a sofa and a bed.
MARK: Right.
LOUISE: The price was good, though. Only $600 a month – much cheaper than the other ones we've looked at so far.

2.
LOUISE: Well, that one had a huge living room.
MARK: Yeah. But it's pretty dark. I guess it doesn't get a lot of light because it's on the ground floor.
LOUISE: I think it'd be noisy, too. It's not a very quiet neighborhood, and there's a lot of traffic.
MARK: I guess that's why it's only $700 a month. The kitchen was pretty small, too. I don't think there's room for a refrigerator.
LOUISE: That'd be a problem. I suppose we could put one in the living room.
MARK: Maybe. I was happy with the bedrooms, though. Two bedrooms would be great. We could use one as a study.

C Listen again. How much is the rent for each apartment? What is the neighborhood like? Complete the chart.

Answer Key
A
Answers will vary.
B
1.
1. T   2. T   3. T   4. F
2.
1. F   2. T   3. T   4. F
C
1. $600; interesting, lively
2. $700; noisy, lots of traffic

Unit 4

Audio Script
How do you make that dish? [Track 4]

B Listen to the conversations at dinner. Number the dishes from 1 to 3.

1.
MAN 1: This is very healthy, and it only takes a few minutes to make.
MAN 2: What kind of vegetables do you use?
MAN 1: You can use almost anything you like. But I like tomatoes, red peppers, bean sprouts, and some onions.
MAN 2: Mmm. Then what?
MAN 1: Well, first, you slice the vegetables into thin pieces.
MAN 2: OK.
MAN 1: After that, you heat a little oil in a frying pan or wok until it's really hot. Then add the vegetables, and stir them until they're lightly cooked.
MAN 2: How long does that take?
MAN 1: Oh, three or four minutes. Don't overcook them! Then you can add some spices, like salt and pepper – or whatever you want, to add flavor. I put in a little soy sauce. And that's about it.

2.
WOMAN: I've never made one of these. Do you make your own, or do you just buy them frozen?
MAN: I like to make my own. Then I can put whatever I like on them.
WOMAN: And do you make the dough for the crust?
MAN: Well, no, actually. I buy that from the supermarket. It's easier. You also need some tomato sauce, some shrimp, and vegetables – like tomatoes and garlic.
WOMAN: How do you start?
MAN: First, spread the dough out into plate-sized pieces to make the crusts. Then sprinkle them with a little olive oil.
WOMAN: OK.
MAN: Then spread your tomato sauce over the dough, add the shrimp and the garlic, and bake for about 20 minutes.

3.
MAN: Have you ever tried making this?
WOMAN: Oh, sure. It's pretty easy, really.
MAN: What do you need?
WOMAN: Well, some ground beef, garlic, onions, and spices. And some bread crumbs.
MAN: What are the bread crumbs for?
WOMAN: They hold the balls together.
MAN: OK. What about the sauce?
WOMAN: Well, I usually just use canned tomato sauce.
MAN: So tell me how you make it.
WOMAN: First, chop up the garlic and onions very finely, and then fry them. Next, mix them with the meat, and add some spices and bread crumbs. After that, you make the meatballs.
MAN: Do they just cook in the sauce?
WOMAN: First, I like to fry them a little until they're brown on the outside. Then cook them in the sauce for about 20 minutes.

C Listen again. Check true or false.

Answer Key
A
Answers will vary.
B
2, 1, 3

C
1.
1. F   2. F   3. T   4. T
2.
1. F   2. T   3. F   4. T
3.
1. F   2. T   3. T   4. F

Unit 5

Audio Script

Summer break [Track 5]

B Listen to John and Maria talk about their summer plans. Check the correct answers.

John
WOMAN: Hey, John. What are you going to do over the summer break?
JOHN: I'm going to work at a special summer camp for inner-city kids. I'm really excited about it.
WOMAN: Why do they have a special camp?
JOHN: Well, because they don't get much chance to get away from the city.
WOMAN: What kind of things do they do there?
JOHN: Let's see. . . . There's kayaking, sports, swimming – and things like that.
WOMAN: And what are you going to do there?
JOHN: I'm going to teach the kids kayaking and take them on hikes.
WOMAN: It sounds like a lot of fun.
JOHN: Yeah! And the best thing is, I get paid for it!
WOMAN: So how long are you going to be away?
JOHN: I'll probably be there for three or four weeks.

Maria
WOMAN: Have you made any vacation plans yet, Maria?
MARIA: Actually, I'm not taking a vacation. I'm going to have a summer internship with an advertising agency.
WOMAN: Wow! Tell me more.
MARIA: Well, I saw this internship advertised on the Internet, so I applied for it. I was kind of surprised when they called me, but it's a great opportunity. I'll be working with a big advertising agency in the city for about six weeks.
WOMAN: Interesting! Will you get paid?
MARIA: No, but I get a meal and travel allowance. And I don't have to work all day. I only need to be there in the mornings. The main thing is, I'll get some really useful experience in case I decide to go into advertising when I graduate.

C Listen again. What is the best thing about each plan? Complete the sentences.

Answer Key

A
Answers will vary.
B
John
1. a   2. b   3. b
Maria
1. b   2. b   3. a
C
1. paid to work and have fun
2. some really useful experience

Unit 6

Audio Script

Noisy neighbors [Track 6]

B Listen to the conversations. Check the people's complaints.

1.
MRS. RIVERA: Hi, Mrs. Lang. It's Mrs. Rivera – your neighbor from the apartment downstairs.
MRS. LANG: Oh, hello.
MRS. RIVERA: I'm sorry to complain, but I wonder if you could ask your kids to make a little less noise.
MRS. LANG: Oh, sorry. I didn't realize. Is it their music? I know they love loud music. I'll ask them to turn it down.
MRS. RIVERA: No, it's not their music. It's their feet. They seem to jump around a lot, and I keep hearing this strange sound. It's kind of a . . . thumping noise.
MRS. LANG: Oh, sorry. I know what that is. It's my daughter, Celine. She's just started ballet lessons, and I guess she's practicing.
MRS. RIVERA: Oh. I see. Well, maybe if she practiced in the afternoon instead of so early in the morning . . .
MRS. LANG: OK. I'll ask her to do that. I'm so sorry she disturbed you.
2.
MR. GREEN: Excuse me, Mr. Roberti. Can I talk to you for a moment? I'm Mr. Green. I moved into the house next door.
MR. ROBERTI: Oh, yes. Hello.
MR. GREEN: I wondered if I could ask a favor.
MR. ROBERTI: Why, certainly. Is it our dog? I hope he hasn't been chasing your cat.
MR. GREEN: No, it's not that. It's your son's friends, I think.
MR. ROBERTI: Really. I know Mike's friends visit him a lot. He's in a band, and they always come here to practice. Is it the noise?
MR. GREEN: No, it's not that. The thing is, sometimes when they visit, they park in front of my driveway, and I can't get my car out. Please ask them not to park there, or I'll have to get them towed away.
MR. ROBERTI: I understand. I'll tell them to use the parking lot down the street. I guess they're just too lazy to walk here from the parking lot. That's teenagers for you!

C Listen again. How do the people solve the problems? Complete the sentences.

Answer Key

A
Answers will vary.
B
1. b   2. b
C
1. practice in the afternoon
2. use the parking lot down the street

Unit 7

Audio Script

What's this for? [Track 7]

B Listen to people talk about the gadgets. Number the pictures from 1 to 3.

1.
MAN: This is great! You can use it to clean the sofa or the inside of your car. It's rechargeable, so it runs for about 30 minutes when it's fully charged. Also, if you drop stuff

on the carpet, it picks up the dirt very easily. It's very light, too, so it's really easy to use. It only has a small bag inside to collect the dirt, so don't forget to change the bag regularly. You can see when it's full through the plastic cover. Be sure to put it back on the charger after you use it, or the battery will run down, and it won't work.

2.

WOMAN: You can use this for storing all your telephone numbers and addresses. It's much easier than writing things in a notebook. And you can write directly on it. Just write names here, addresses on this part, and telephone numbers here. It reads your handwriting and turns it into print. But make sure that you write neatly, or it may not be able to read your writing. Here's the great thing: it holds up to 1,000 names and addresses!

3.

WOMAN: This is very convenient. You can use it to cook all sorts of things, like meat and vegetables. It cooks them very slowly. You put the food inside and then choose the cooking time. You can program it to turn on and off for exactly when you want it to cook. So you can set it up before you go to work, and then everything will be ready when you get home. Make sure it has enough liquid in it, though.

C Listen again. Check true or false.

Answer Key

A
Answers will vary.

B
1, 3, 2

C
1.
1. F   2. F   3. T
2.
1. F   2. F   3. F
3.
1. T   2. T   3. F

Unit 8

Audio Script

Party time! [Track 8]

B Listen to people talk about different celebrations. Number the pictures from 1 to 3.

1.

MAN: When any of us has a birthday, the rule is that we all go out together. We like to get a nice present and treat the birthday person to dinner at a restaurant. But it's nice just to get together. We've been doing this now for over ten years – ever since we became friends at college. It's a way to keep in touch, and a time to catch up on what's been happening with everyone.

2.

WOMAN: For Thanksgiving, we usually like to get together with some of the neighbors for a big dinner. We take turns having it at each other's homes. It's fun because it's a time when the guys do all the cooking. But the menu is always the same – roast turkey with stuffing and mashed potatoes. After a fabulous dinner, we watch a football game together on TV.

3.

WOMAN: At the end of the school year – before everyone goes off on vacation – my classmates like to have a picnic.

We go to a nice place by the river, and everyone brings something to eat. It's a time when we talk about our plans for the summer. Usually it's nice and warm, and we all like to go swimming in the river.

C Listen again. Complete the chart.

Answer Key

A
Answers will vary.

B
3, 2, 1

C
1. birthday; college friends; go out to dinner together
2. Thanksgiving; neighbors; get together for dinner
3. end of the school year; classmates; have a picnic

Unit 9

Audio Script

Future plans [Track 9]

B Listen to four people talk about possible plans for the summer. Check the plans they are considering.

Stan

STAN: I really should study it during the summer vacation. It's a skill I really need. And these days, every time you apply for a job, they expect you to be good at it. But if I do it, I won't be able to go away with my parents on the camping trip. That's something we do every summer, and I really love it.

Janet

JANET: I've been thinking about learning it for a long time. It's really very useful, especially if you're traveling in Central or South America. My friend speaks it pretty well and said it wasn't that difficult to learn. But if I do it, I'll have to take classes every evening, which is the only time I'm free. And then I won't be able to see my boyfriend as much, and I don't think he'd like that.

Tammy

TAMMY: I used to be in much better shape, but I stopped playing tennis last year. Since then, I've gotten really lazy. I used to go twice a week, and I've been thinking of starting to go again. It would really help me stay in shape and have more energy. But if I do it, I'll have to buy a car because the nearest one is really far away from our house.

Stuart

STUART: It's probably about time I thought seriously about it. It would be great to have children, and I know it would make my parents happy. And I don't really enjoy living by myself. But if I do it, I'll have to get a better job because the one I have now doesn't pay enough for two people to live on.

C Listen again. What are the negative consequences of each plan? Complete the sentences.

Answer Key

A
Answers will vary.

B
Stan: b   Tammy: a
Janet: b   Stuart: a

C
1. go camping with his parents   3. buy a car
2. see her boyfriend as much   4. get a better job

D
Answers will vary.

Unit 10

Audio Script

The right job [Track 10]

B Listen to people talk about the answers from their questionnaires. Check the jobs they are describing.

1.

WOMAN: It would be a good job for me because I like helping people. I think I'm pretty patient, and I understand how people think and feel. It would be very rewarding to help people with their problems. However, the thing I don't like about it is that it could be pretty stressful at times. I'm not sure how I would deal with that.

2.

MAN: I think I'm pretty creative – I always have ideas that I would like to turn into stories. I also love thinking about relationships and how people react in different situations. It's very difficult to get started and to get your work published, though, so I would probably need to have another job as well.

3.

MAN: I have a background in art, so I think I can tell when something looks good. I studied computers as well, so I know quite a lot about it. I've seen a lot of bad sites, and I think I know what's needed to make a really good one. However, so many people are doing this kind of thing that it's become very, very competitive, and it's hard to get good contracts.

4.

WOMAN: I think the work would be interesting – and also very rewarding. When you see people making progress, you get a sense of doing something worthwhile. I think I'd do well working with sick children because I love kids and get along really well with them. The thing I wouldn't like would be shift work. Sometimes you'd have to work all night.

C Listen again. What is the problem with each job? Complete the sentences.

Answer Key

A
Answers will vary.

B
1. b   2. a   3. b   4. a

C
1. pretty stressful at times
2. get your work published
3. very competitive
4. work all night

Unit 11

Audio Script

Places to see [Track 11]

B Listen to a tour guide talk about the places. Number the pictures from 1 to 3.

1.

TOUR GUIDE: This is a nice part of the city to relax in. I often come here for a walk on the weekend. It's a great place to listen to the birds and smell the flowers. It looks as if it's been here for years, but actually it was only opened a couple of years ago. There used to be lots of old factories here, but the city decided to tear them all down because we didn't have enough green space in the city.

2.

TOUR GUIDE: This is the tallest building in the city. It's over 50 stories high. It was finished two years ago. The top 20 floors are a hotel, and there's a restaurant at the top with a fantastic view of the city. In fact, on a clear day, you can see for 80 kilometers or more.

3.

TOUR GUIDE: This was built for our local baseball and football teams. It has that unusual color because it's made entirely of steel. It can hold over 30,000 people. It can be used all year round because it has a special roof that closes when the weather is bad. It was opened ten years ago.

C Listen again. Complete the sentences.

Answer Key

A
Answers will vary.

B
2, 3, 1

C
1. a couple of; relax; walk; listen to birds; smell flowers
2. two; 50; restaurant; 80
3. ten; baseball; football; 30,000

D
Answers will vary.

Unit 12

Audio Script

Success stories [Track 12]

B Listen to three interviews with successful people. Check the correct information.

1.

INTERVIEWER: Was it difficult to get started as an artist?

MAN: Yes. It's not easy to sell your work when you first start out. I didn't sell anything the first year. Most people don't spend a lot of money on art. Luckily, a few years after I graduated from art school, a buyer from a big gallery in Los Angeles saw my work and asked me to send them some paintings. They sold really well, and since then, my work has become pretty well known on the West Coast.

2.

INTERVIEWER: So how did you get started as a nightclub singer?

WOMAN: Well, I was always a good singer as a child, even though no one in my family was musical. I used to sing in school choirs and things. Anyway, I was singing in a college concert, and an agent heard me and asked me to join a show on Broadway.

INTERVIEWER: A musical?

WOMAN: That's right. I sang in the chorus for about six months. Then one day, the star got sick, and I was asked to sing the lead role. After that, I got sort of famous, and that's when my career really took off. But what I really want to do is record my own album.

3.

INTERVIEWER: Were you always interested in starting a food business?

MAN: Actually, I was interested in sales at first because that's what both my parents do. But I used to work part-time in a café when I was a kid, and that's what got me interested.

INTERVIEWER: What was the first place you opened?
MAN: I started selling sandwiches and stuff. I rented a cheap place near the university, and I started selling lunches to the students. The place was always crowded at lunchtime. So, one day this guy came in and offered me a lot of money for the business. So I sold it! And with that money, I opened a much bigger place downtown.

C Listen again. Complete the sentences.

Answer Key

A
Answers will vary.
B
1. b   2. b   3. b
C
1. a buyer from a big gallery saw his work
2. the star got sick
3. opened a bigger place downtown

Unit 13

Audio Script

Let's rent a movie! [Track 13]

B Listen to three conversations about movies. Check true or false.

1.
WOMAN: What's that?
MAN: It's an old mystery movie I rented.
WOMAN: Oh, I love those! What's this one about?
MAN: It's about a group of people who go on a sailing trip. But there's a murderer on board the boat because passengers keep getting killed.
WOMAN: Oh, yeah? And have you figured out who's doing it yet?
MAN: Not really, but I think it might be the captain.
WOMAN: And how's the movie so far?
MAN: It's getting pretty scary. Want to watch it with me?

2.
WOMAN: Have you rented any good videos lately?
MAN: I rented a great documentary last night. It's a true story about this guy who sailed a boat around the world on his own. He was only 18. It's unbelievable – and really well done.
WOMAN: Amazing.
MAN: Yeah. He ran into a few big storms, and his boat overturned a couple of times, but he managed to survive.
WOMAN: How long did it take him?
MAN: It took him 11 weeks altogether.
WOMAN: Incredible.

3.
WOMAN: Have you seen this one yet? It's got my favorite actor in it. He's so gorgeous!
MAN: Yeah, I saw it last week. But it's not one of his best movies, I'm afraid.
WOMAN: What's it about?
MAN: It's a love story. It's about how these two people meet by chance on a flight from New York to London, and then they don't see each other again for five years. By then, they're both in unhappy marriages, so of course, everything starts getting complicated. But the story is kind of strange, and the characters aren't very believable.
WOMAN: Thanks for warning me. I'll look for something else.

C Listen again. Check the word that best describes each movie.

Answer Key

A
Answers will vary.
B
1.
1. F   2. T   3. T
2.
1. F   2. T   3. T
3.
1. F   2. F   3. T
C
1. suspenseful   2. interesting   3. disappointing

Unit 14

Audio Script

Did you see that? [Track 14]

B Listen to conversations about the gestures. Number the pictures from 1 to 3.

1.
WOMAN: So how did it go in Buenos Aires, Jason?
JASON: Great! Well, . . . there was this one little incident.
WOMAN: What happened?
JASON: I was in a business meeting when the phone rang. Mr. Gomez answered, and then he looked right at me and started turning his finger around in little circles – up here, by his forehead.
WOMAN: You're kidding! So what did you do?
JASON: I got upset. I felt insulted. There he was making signals at me like I was crazy. But . . .
WOMAN: But what?
JASON: I found out that in Argentina, it means you have a telephone call.

2.
MRS. JOHNSON: Did you see that? What did she think I was going to do – hurt her daughter?
WOMAN: What's wrong, Mrs. Johnson?
MRS. JOHNSON: That dear little girl – she's so cute! She reminded me of my own daughter. So I was patting her on the head, and her mother quickly pulled her away.
WOMAN: Well, actually, what you did is not considered polite here, Mrs. Johnson.
MRS. JOHNSON: What? What do you mean?
WOMAN: It's very impolite to touch people on the head here.
MRS. JOHNSON: Oh, I didn't know that!

3.
WOMAN: Do you know that guy in the front row?
MARTY: Who? Which guy?
WOMAN: There! See that guy? He keeps holding up his hand and waving it at you. And he's got his thumb and his little finger sticking out. . . . Weird.
MARTY: Oh, that's my friend, Don. That signal means "relax." He knows I'm really nervous about singing a solo.
WOMAN: OK. If you say so.

C Listen again. Check true or false.

Answer Key

A
Answers will vary.
B
2, 3, 1

C
1.
1. T 2. F 3. T
2.
1. F 2. F 3. T
3.
1. T 2. T 3. T
D
Answers will vary.

Unit 15

Audio Script

What would you do? [Track 15]

B Listen to three people talk about different situations. Check the two words that best describe each person's feelings.

1.
WOMAN: I was driving with a friend in the countryside last weekend when I saw a little puppy on the side of the road. There weren't any houses nearby, and the dog seemed to be lost. I was worried it might get run over, so I stopped the car and went to check it out. The puppy seemed to be really scared and very hungry, too. I think someone must have left it there. Maybe they didn't want it anymore. Some people are so cruel!

2.
MAN: The other day I saw a guy acting pretty strangely. It was about ten o'clock at night, and he was standing behind a tree watching my neighbor's house. He probably thought nobody could see him because it was dark, but I noticed him when I took my dog out for a walk. As soon as he saw me, he hid behind the tree. I pretended that I hadn't seen him.

3.
WOMAN: One of my friends invited me to see a movie with her last week. I was sure she'd said Wednesday night, and I wrote it down on my calendar as Wednesday. On Tuesday night, I didn't come home until late because I had decided to go to a friend's house and watch a video. When I got home, there was an angry message on my answering machine from my friend. Our appointment was for Tuesday night, and she'd waited for me in front of the theater for an hour.

C Listen again. Check what each person probably did next.

Answer Key

A
Answers will vary.
B
1. concerned, disgusted
2. puzzled, worried
3. surprised, embarrassed
C
1. b 2. a 3. b

Unit 16

Audio Script

What's your excuse? [Track 16]

B Listen to four invitations. Complete the chart.

1.
ERICA: Hi, Jane. This is Erica.
JANE: Hello, Erica. How are things?
ERICA: Just great, thanks. Say, I was wondering if you'd like to come to a barbecue.
JANE: A barbecue! That sounds really good. When is it?
ERICA: On Sunday afternoon.
JANE: Sure, I'm free then. And where's it going to be?
ERICA: It'll be at my place.
JANE: Great. Thanks. It sounds wonderful.

2.
JIM: Hi, Rick.
RICK: Oh, hi, Jim. What's up?
JIM: Well, the reason I'm calling is about a rock concert. Interested?
RICK: A rock concert. Umm. When is it?
JIM: It's this Friday night, at the Music Hall.
RICK: Gee. I'd really love to go, but I've got a date.
JIM: Too bad. Well, enjoy your date.
RICK: And you enjoy the concert.

3.
SUZANNE: Hi, Elena. It's Suzanne.
ELENA: Hi, Suzanne. How are you?
SUZANNE: Good, thanks. Elena, did you know it's Sandra's birthday on Sunday?
ELENA: Is it? That's nice.
SUZANNE: Yes. We're planning a surprise party for her at my place. Can you come?
ELENA: Sure, I'd love to. I love surprise parties!

4.
JENNY: Hi, Ryan. This is Jenny.
RYAN: Hi, Jenny. How have you been?
JENNY: Pretty good. And you?
RYAN: Yeah, things are good.
JENNY: Say, I have two tickets to a baseball game this Saturday afternoon at the stadium. Would you be interested in going?
RYAN: Wow. I'd love to, but unfortunately I promised to help my brother move on Saturday. He has a ton of stuff to move to his new place, so he really needs my help.
JENNY: No problem.

C Listen again. Check whether the people accept or refuse. If they refuse, write the excuse.

Answer Key

A
Answers will vary.

B
1. barbecue; Sunday afternoon; Erica's place
2. rock concert; Friday night; the Music Hall
3. surprise birthday party; Sunday; Suzanne's place
4. baseball game; Saturday afternoon; the stadium

C
1. accept
2. refuse; has a date
3. accept
4. refuse; has to help his brother move

ANSWER KEY *GRAMMAR*

Unit 1

1 *From Mexico to Brazil*

1. Where was
2. When did
3. Were his
4. Where did they
5. Did he go
6. What did he

2 *When you were younger . . .*

A
Answers will vary.

Unit 2

1 *Street interview*

Maria: less / more
Maria: enough / many / much / enough

2 *The tourist*

Answers will vary.

Unit 3

1 *Moving houses*

not big enough / too dark / not as convenient as /
not enough / too expensive

2 *The wish game*

A
Answers will vary.

Unit 4

1 *A pizza recipe*

A/B
  2   Then bake the dough for five minutes.
  3   After that, take the dough out of the oven.
  4   Next, spread tomato sauce over the dough.
  1   First, roll out the dough into a circle.
  6   Finally, bake the pizza in a preheated oven until
      the cheese melts.

2 *Food experiences*

A
Answers will vary.

Unit 5

1 *Sunday plans*

B: am going to
B: will
A: Are / going to
B: will / is going to / will
A: will

2 *What should I do?*

Answers will vary.

Unit 6

1 *Requests*

2. on
3. up
4. out
5. up
6. up
7. out
8. off
9. away
10. on

2 *Responding to requests*

Answers will vary.

Unit 7

1 *Computer technology*

2. are used for
3. is used for
4. is used to
5. is used for
6. are used for
7. are used to
8. are used to
9. is used to
10. is used for

2 *Guessing game*

A
Answers will vary.

Unit 8

1 *Special days*

2. Fall is the season when some trees change colors.
3. Summer is a time of year when many people go to
   the beach.
4. A honeymoon is a time when a bride and groom go
   on vacation together.
5. March is the month when spring begins in the
   northern hemisphere.
6. January 1 is the day when some people make New
   Year's resolutions.

2 *Quiz*

A
Answers will vary.
B
Answers will vary.

Unit 9

1 *What will happen?*

Answers will vary.

2 *Our changing world*

A
Answers will vary.

Photocopiable

Unit 10

1 How about you?

2. Neither do I.; Well, I do.
3. Neither can I.; Really? I like it. (*or* Oh, I don't mind.)
4. So am I.; Gee, I'm not.
5. So am I.; Gee, I'm not.
6. Neither am I.; I am!

2 The best candidate

A
Answers will vary.

Unit 11

1 Did you know . . . ?

2. Alaska was sold by Russia to the United States in the 1860s.
3. The Suez Canal was constructed by Egyptian workers in the 1860s.
4. Yellowstone Park was created by the U.S. government in 1872.
5. The Eiffel Tower was designed by French architect Gustave Eiffel.

2 Currencies and languages

A
Answers will vary.

Unit 12

1 Unforgettable moments

1. had / got / were cooking / heard / opened / found
2. were ice-skating / met / fell / was looking
3. saw / were traveling
4. were watching / rang

2 What have you been doing lately?

A
Answers will vary.

Unit 13

1 How did you like it?

Mike: fascinating
Linda: interesting
Mike: surprised
Mike: amazing

2 Your favorites

A
Answers will vary.

Unit 14

1 May I?

A
Permission: are allowed to / can
Obligation: have got to / have to
Prohibition: aren't allowed to / can't

B
2. You can't park your car here.
3. You can camp here.
4. You have got to wear shoes. (*or* You've got to wear shoes.)
5. You have to wear your seat belt.
6. You aren't allowed to chew gum in class. (*or* You're not allowed to chew gum in class.)

2 Strange happenings

Answers will vary.

Unit 15

1 What would you do?

Answers will vary.

2 What would you have done?

Answers will vary.

Unit 16

1 Don't forget to . . .

2. The teacher said to study the new words in the article.
3. The teacher asked us not to look up every new word in the dictionary.
4. The teacher asked us to bring a newspaper to class.
5. The teacher said not to read the newspaper before class.
6. The teacher told us not to be late for class.

2 What an excuse!

A
Answers will vary.

Unit 1

2 *Practice*

A/B/C
Answers will vary.

Unit 2

2 *Practice*

A/B
Answers will vary.

Unit 3

2 *Practice*

A/B/C
Answers will vary.

Unit 4

2 *Practice*

A/B
Answers will vary.

Unit 5

2 *Practice*

A/B/C
Answers will vary.

Unit 6

2 *Practice*

A/B/C
Answers will vary.

Unit 7

2 *Practice*

A/B/C
Answers will vary.

Unit 8

2 *Practice*

A/B
Answers will vary.

Unit 9

2 *Practice*

A/B
Answers will vary.

Unit 10

2 *Practice*

A/B/C
Answers will vary.

Unit 11

2 *Practice*

A/B
Answers will vary.

Unit 12

2 *Practice*

A
Answers will vary.

Unit 13

2 *Practice*

A/B
Answers will vary.

Unit 14

2 *Practice*

A/B
Answers will vary.

Unit 15

2 *Practice*

A/B/C
Answers will vary.

Unit 16

2 *Practice*

A
Answers will vary.

B
2. offer help
3. give an excuse
4. express concern
5. make a criticism
6. give advice
7. tell a joke
8. make an invitation

C
Answers will vary.

ANSWER KEY WRITING

Unit 1

① Before you write

2. Announcement, Education, Work experience, Welcome

Unit 2

① Before you write

_2_ few traffic lights	_7_ many cars on road
_3_ few safe crossings	_8_ many traffic jams
_4_ dangerous	_9_ more noise
_5_ slow traffic	_10_ more pollution
_6_ few bus lines	

Unit 3

① Before you write

Advantages: new, in a nice area, not as expensive as old place
Disadvantages: smaller than old place, not as many windows, not enough closets
Wishes: bigger living room, more space for furniture, didn't have to sell sofa

Unit 4

① Before you write

A
2. c   3. e   4. b   5. a

Unit 5

① Before you write

2. possible plan   5. advice
3. possible plan   6. advice
4. plan

Unit 6

① Before you write

A
1. c   2. a   3. b
B
2. take out garbage tomorrow; collector only comes twice a week
3. put things back in refrigerator; had to throw away milk

Unit 7

① Before you write

Items *1*, *2*, and *3* are about the house.
Items *4*, *5*, and *6* are about the neighborhood.

Unit 8

① Before you write

Answers will vary.

Unit 9

① Before you write

A
Answers will vary.
B
2. Accept the offer.; You will feel less secure.
3. Ask for time to think about it.; Someone else may get the job.

Unit 10

① Before you write

1. a   2. a   3. b   4. Answers will vary.

Unit 11

① Before you write

A
1. History
2. Attractions
3. Location
B
1. was built; was opened; was damaged; were killed; wasn't damaged
2. is visited
3. is located

Unit 12

① Before you write

_3_ request for an interview
_1_ job he's applying for
_2_ relevant experience

Unit 13

① Before you write

1. Title, Author, Plot, Reviewer's opinions

Unit 14

① Before you write

1. c, e   2. a, f   3. b, d

Unit 15

① Before you write

1. Bob
2. Andrea
3. Andrea

Unit 16

① Before you write

2. to ask for information
3. to make an offer
4. to give a warning
5. to invite
6. to ask for a favor